The
Last
Adventure

Other books by Marcel LaPerriere

Just Another Adventure

The Adventure Continues

and

The Road to Adventure

The
Last
Adventure

Living with Amyotrophic Lateral Sclerosis (ALS)

By
Marcel LaPerriere

Published by Marcel LaPerriere, 2022
Printed in the United States of America
Distributed by Ingram Spark
ISBN: 979-8-218-06345-0

Book design: Dana G. Anderson
Editors: Bonnie and Max Cotrell

The events and experiences that follow are all true, based on the author's recollection of them. In some situations, names, identities, and other specifics of individuals have been changed in order to protect their privacy.

Dedication

To all pALS and cALS around the world

pALS, PALS, or Pals:

Person, patient, or people with ALS

cALS, CALS, or Cals:

Caregiver of anyone living with ALS

Note: Throughout this book, other books, or online, you are apt to see the above abbreviations when talking about ALS and caregivers who care for people living with ALS. I've noticed even medical folks are starting to use these abbreviations.

Table of Contents

Introduction

As my two cave diving partners and I began the long ascent out of the cave, I glanced down to see my depth gauge read 266 feet: over twice the safe sport diving depth. You may already be questioning my sanity, or be ready to call me an adrenaline junky. I have always loved living literally on the edge, so it would be hard for me to argue, especially about the crazy part. I said literally on the edge because more times than I can remember when climbing, I found myself on a lofty perch with nothing but air to my left or my right. There was little to keep me from cratering into the ground 2000 feet or more below. More than once, I've forced my body through such tight places in both dry and underwater caves that I've had to take my helmet off and push it ahead of me to fit. Am I totally bonkers? Maybe I am.

I've also been attracted to jobs that stimulate both my creativity and adrenaline production. Jobs like inspecting a 200-yard-long underwater tunnel that supplies water to a hydroelectric powerplant via scuba diving.

Or scaling (prying) large rocks off a near-vertical cliff above a hydroelectric dam spillway while dangling from the end of a rope no bigger than my pinky finger. It's darn fun while hanging at the end of such a rope to use the hydraulic jack to dislodge a rock as big as a minivan and see it tumble down a 50-foot cliff. I can also guarantee high adrenaline-flow when you're standing on the edge of a dam while a helicopter with a 200-foot-long cable hanging under its belly brings you a trip bucket with a ton of concrete in it. One mistake by either the helicopter pilot or you, and you'd be smashed like a bug. One time I climbed a 200-foot radio tower in a windstorm to change the flashing red light on top. And another time I hauled windows for a house my company was building in the bed of my pickup on a remote island with no real roads? As I drove off the landing craft that was bobbing up and down in the surf, I wondered how I would explain the loss of my truck with several thousand dollars of windows to my insurance company. Fortunately, I didn't have to, but I was packed full of adrenaline that day. Only 4-wheel drive and a dedicated crew saved the truck and possibly me from a watery grave when the truck's back end fell off the ramp and landed in 3-feet of saltwater as I drove it back onto the landing craft.

In 1994, I was pulling myself against a strong current into an underwater Florida cave. Photo courtesy of Alan Murray.

I liked playing and working on the edge but never considered myself an adrenaline junky. Maybe I was? Now when my bulbar ALS causes me to choke and adrenaline starts flowing, it's not much fun. When that happens, I am often overcome with the feeling of doom, and I panic. Not much fun at all. However, when the feeling of doom passes, I'm just as ecstatic to be alive as when I freed myself from being good and stuck during a cave dive.

See why I chose the title of *Just Another Adventure* for my first book about living with ALS? And why the second book is titled, *The Adventure Continues*? Knowing this is going to be my last book about living with ALS, I figured *The Last Adventure* fit. Both for the book title and living with ALS will be the last adventure I face while living. I'd rather be taking part in almost any other adventure than ALS, but I'll do my best to face ALS as just another adventure.

September 2014. In the via ferrata, France. Photos courtesy of Jörg Wiltz.

My lovely wife, Connie, follows me onto a cable-suspension bridge.

Marcel in France on via ferrata.

The Construction Tips Appendix. My expertise designing, creating, repairing and constructing machinery and buildings has served me and my wife well since ALS has entered our lives. This appendix is based on posts I made about home modifications on various ALS support sites and a group page I started dedicated to handicap accessibility modifications.

There is nothing more important than staying positive while making the most of bad situations. A big part of staying happy and positive I owe to Connie, my wife. And since she makes me happy, I'm going to treat you to one of her many drawings that always makes me smile. This drawing hangs by our front door and as I get ready to go out into the world, as I struggle to change from my inside wheelchair to my outside wheelchair, I look up and smile at this happy drawing. Because we have a collection of her bird drawings, we're including quite a few in the last section of this book.

A happy puffin walks in the soft grass.

Timeline

Approximate Date	Approximate Age	Symptoms
January 2014	61	Started noticing that my voice would sort of slur or break in the evenings.
August 2014	61 1/2	Connie noticed for the first time that I was slurring my voice.
October 2014	61 3/4	After visiting with our family doctor, we were sent to see a neurologist at Virginia Mason. I started confusing words when I spoke -- simple things like saying bird when I wanted to say seagull.
November 2014	61 3/4	Neurologist suggested that I possibly had primary progressive aphasia. Meanwhile I continued to loose my voice. I entered what I call the drunk phase, because I sounded drunk when I talked.
February 2015	62	Neurologist said that she was fairly sure I had primary progressive aphasia.
March 2015	62	Neurologist suggested that I might have spasmodic dysphonia.

Approximate Date	Approximate Age	Symptoms
April 2015	62	Neurologist Dr. Elliot suggested that I be tested for acromegaly.
June 2015	62 1/2	Acromegaly was confirmed.
July 2015	62 1/2	Met with an endocrinologist, because my tongue was growing. She put me on a three times per day injection of a drug called Octreotide.
August 2015	62 1/2	Started the Octreotide injections and they made me very sick. I was sick for the whole month and my voice got weaker and weaker. The tongue started to shrink.
September 2015	62 1/2	Had an infusion of Sandostatin Depot. That, too, made me sick. The tongue continued to shrink back to normal size. My voice continued to fade away.
October 2015	62 3/4	Had surgery to remove the tumor on my pituitary gland.
October 2015	62 3/4	Bad reaction to penicillin caused erythema multiforme. I ended up in the hospital for a week –– four days in critical care.
January 2016	63	Balance was getting bad.
January 2016	63	Voice –– totally gone.
February 2016	63	Dr. Elliott suggested that I might have pseudobulbar palsy.
February 2016	63	Walking okay, but breathing was becoming more and more labored.
July 2017	64 1/2	Balance issues were found to be from a disorder called semicircular canal dehiscence.
Summer 2017	64	Walking became harder and harder. Started using a walker off and on.
Fall 2017	64 3/4	Started having problems with constipation.
February 2018	65	Attended an ALS Clinic. My ankles were very swollen. Ended up in the ER at Virginia Mason and two nights in the hospital.
March 2018	65	Had a PEG feeding tube installed.
March 2018	65	Walking declined to the point that I ended up in a wheelchair.
April 2018	65 1/4	Started process to get an electric wheelchair.
April 2018	65 1/4	Bedsores started to become an issue.

Approximate Date	Approximate Age	Symptoms
May 2018	65 1/4	A mysterious bedsore with broken skin formed right behind my right big toe.
June 2018	65 1/2	Measured for a power wheelchair on the 13th of June.
June 2018	65 1/2	June 18th, purchased a newly converted, slightly-used 2017 handicap van. Will be delivered in Aug. 2018.
June 2018	65 1/2	Got a new electric wheelchair.
July 2018	65 1/2	Noticed that I was losing more and more dexterity in my fingers, especially on the left hand.
October 2018	65 3/4	I noticed I was having troubles with my eye lids not opening up as they should.
November 2019	65 3/4	Breathing was getting hard and harder. Started the process to get a noninvasive ventilator called a Trilogy Ventilator.
Feb-19	66	Lots of fasciculations at night, mostly on my left side, elbow, kneecap, calf, and my left hand's thumb, index finger and middle finger.
February 2019	66	Swallowing was getting harder. Even ice cream or applesauce was hard to swallow.
March 2019	66	Noted when I slept on my right side in the fetal position, then tried to straighten my right leg that I needed to use my arms to push the leg straight.
April 2019	66 1/4	I could no longer ignore that my neck was getting weak. It was often sore, I had a hard time nodding, "Yes," but could still can shake it "no."
May 2019	66 1/4	Received my Trilogy machine as breathing continued to get harder.
May 2019	66 1/4	Noticed that my toes were curling under. Especially bad on the left side.
August 2019	66 1/2	Had eyebrow lift surgery.
September 2019	66 1/2	Left toes were curled to the point that the two longest toes totally curled under.
September 2019	66 1/2	Noticed that my left hand fingers were seizing up. They locked straight out. I had to straighten them with my other hand.
October 2019	66 1/2	Started using a power wheelchair inside the house.

Approximate Date	Approximate Age	Symptoms
November 2019	66 3/4	Came to the point I had to admit that for the last few months my hands had been experiencing tremors. The tremors were getting worse and mostly happened in my left hand.
January 2020	67	A skin ulcer formed on my left shin. It was about 1 1/2 inches in diameter with an open area in the middle about the diameter of a pencil eraser. After trying a few ointments, the thing that healed the sore was dabbing honey on the ulcer.
January 2020	67	Both heels were experiencing pain on the bottoms. Possibly caused by poor circulation?
March 2020	67	Started needing to use the Hoyer lift to get into bed.
March 2020	67	Shaved my beard for the first time in over 30 years.
April 2020	67	Started getting supplemental nutrition via the feeding tube.
November 2020	67 3/4	A urologist suggested I likely have a neurogenic bladder which is causing me to slowly void my bladder.
January 2021	68	Another urologist confirmed the neurogenic bladder caused by ALS.
February 2021	68	Started wearing a neck brace when going outside.

Essays

Classical Homework

16 June 2019

Last night, during intermission, our friend Bonnie Cottrell asked me if I'd ever written a story about why I like classical music. I shook my head "no," and she told me I should. I gave her thumbs up that I would, and she then said, "That's your homework assignment." Well, in the days of my youth, I would have put that assignment off until the last second, but nowadays, I'm not particularly eager to procrastinate. So, here it goes.

I could be snarky and just type 'I don't know, I've always liked classical music." However, I'll try to do a better job than that.

I can honestly say it wasn't because of my parents. My mother died when I was seven, and I only remember her practicing on her organ for the music she was going to play in church. Sadly, I don't know what kind of music she liked. But my father liked the music sung by the crooners of that era, the likes of Bing Crosby, Frank Sinatra, Dean Martin, John Gary, and Dennis Day. In fact, my middle name is Dennis because my dad loved his music.

Marcel LaPerriere

You won't find me saying many good things about my father, but one is that he was an excellent singer. He liked to learn all the songs that the crooners sung, especially the Irish songs like "Toora Loora Loora," "Danny Boy," "Cockles and Mussels," and many more. To learn those songs, with all the proper pauses and inflections, he'd sometimes stand in front of the hi-fi stereo, and each time a song would end on the LP record, he'd place the needle back at the beginning of the song and start it over, sometimes singing along, sometimes not.

The first 45 RPM record I purchased was Gary Puckett and the Union Gap, singing "Young Girl." And, I think it was the one and only rock and roll record I ever purchased. When I was fourteen and lived with my aunt and uncle for a bit over a year, my cousin, Charles, and I bought more than one Bill Cosby album, and we teens would sit around listing to them over and over again. We'd laugh at each funny line on the record, even though we'd heard the same joke more than once. We also listened to Casey Kasem on the radio counting down the Top 40 Hits of the Week.

As an older teen, when I went to live with my brother, Fred, and his wife, Kay, I don't remember listening to a lot of music. When riding to and from work with Fred, mostly a half-hour to an hour each way depending on traffic, we'd mostly listen to the news on the AM radio. During that time I purchased my first LP record of Richard Strauss' symphonies and a record of Beethoven's 5th Symphony. Kay and I'd sometimes listen to those records and other classical music when Fred was working late. Kay would be baking or cooking dinner, and I'd be reading a book, most likely about a mountain climbing adventure. Maybe it was Kay who cemented my love of classical music? Even as a teenager I'd much rather listen to classical music than rock. When I got my first car, I had the first push selector tuned to a classical station and the others set to rock stations. When one of my friends was riding in the car with me, we'd listen to rock, but as soon as they were gone, I'd push that first button and go back to listen to classical. That was weird for a teen in the early '70s.

When Connie, who already loved classical music, and I were first dating, we were much too poor to afford a stereo or even a cheap record player for our first apartment in Nebraska. Heck, we couldn't even afford a radio. We only listened to music when we were driving in our ragtop 1962 Jeep and the best we could find was country and western. We both hated what was commonly called "shit kicking music." Once, we were extra excited when we heard that a music professor at Connie's college was giving a free piano concert featuring pieces by Chopin. We were very disappointed when we found out that he couldn't play the piano much better than a typical first-year piano student. And to make things worse, out of politeness his audience clapped, and he played two encores. That was the worst music experience of our lives. The best thing about it: nearly fifty years later I can now laugh at how bad he was.

When we moved to Seattle, we were still much too poor to afford any device that would supply us with music. I worked as an apprentice machinist, and any extra money had to be used to buy the tools needed for my trade. To supplement our meager income, Connie got a job sewing square dance dresses, and her bosses, a wife and husband team, took pity on her and gave us an AM radio. Thinking about that radio still makes me laugh because the tuner was broken, or more correctly, the belt from the knob to the tuner was broken. To try to fix the problem I put a rubber band from the knob to the tuner. My fix sort of worked, but when you'd find the station you wanted and lift your fingers off the knob, the radio would slowly drift out of tune. The trick was to try and stop turning the knob about a ¼ turn before the station you wanted and cross your fingers that the station would come into tune. We learned not to change the station on our "rubber band radio." Eventually, that radio got stuck on one soft rock station, and to this day, when I hear Roberta Flack singing "Killing Me Softly," I'm transported to 1973 and our little apartment.

Besides being an excellent place to work and learn, the company where I served my apprenticeship allowed us to listen to the radio. I first shared the machine shop area with a journeyman machinist named Don. He was forty years older, the senior employee, and had the radio tuned to a station that played music from the '30s and '40s, which was mostly to my liking. That station played songs like "Boogie Woogie Bugle Boy," "I'll Never Smile Again," "Walking My Baby Back Home," and many more. But never any classical. When Don retired, I quickly turned to KING FM, which was and still is a magnificent classical station. Fortunately, when Don was replaced by a very nice man named John, we compromised. Some days we'd listen to KING FM, and somedays we'd listen to music Don liked. Then came Roger, and he too loved KING FM, so the station stayed there, or we'd listen to jazz on the new public radio station KUOW. When KUOW started daily playing *Radio Reader*, featuring Dick Estell reading from popular books of the day, Roger and I became fans. Each day, just before 10:00, we'd be sure to turn the dial to KUOW and turn the volume up so we could hear him reading over the clatter of the machines we were running. Roger and I became total *Radio Reader* addicts, and we looked forward to our daily *Radio Reader* fix. However, as soon as we got our fix satisfied, we'd turn back to KING FM. One afternoon each week KING would feature an opera, and I'm guessing that's when my love for opera was born.

Sometime during our married life, Connie and I owned an 8-track cassette player, and it was not easy to find classical music in that format. Eight-track was short-lived, and by the time it and cassette tapes were phased out and replaced by CDs, we were total classical music nerds. That's why in the mid-'80s, when we started finishing the interior of our boat, *Terra Nova*, the first area I built was the place our CD stereo player lived. Then, when we saw an unbelievable sale on a hundred classical music CDs, we jumped on it. In the 21 years we lived on *Terra Nova*, it's hard to recall many waking hours when the CD player wasn't softly playing some piece of classical music. After listening to those one hundred CDs and others multiple times, Brahms became my favorite composer. And my passion for opera deepened, especially when our son Zach gave us a recording of the famous soprano Kiri Te Kanawa when he returned from a year in New Zealand as an exchange student.

Today as I type on the computer, I almost always have opera, choral music, or some other classical music playing. I do like some rock songs from my youth, and unlike Connie, I like jazz, which she tolerates. Both of us gag when we hear much of what the kids listen to today, and we both still dislike shit-kicking music, with a few exceptions like Willie Nelson or Johnny Cash. Give me a Puccini opera, a Brahms Hungarian dance, a Beethoven Symphony, or a Mozart string quartet, and I'll blissfully fill a day typing away at my computer. As much as I hate ALS, I know good music helps me keep the blues away.

Getting Harder

3 July 2019

With one exception, everything gets harder to do. That exception: it's getting easier to see what a wretched disease ALS is. However, even living with ALS, my spirits are mostly good, and I still enjoy life.

It's now been around three-and-a-half years since I could talk and over five years since I first noticed that I was losing my ability to speak. Five years ago, neither we nor the medical folks knew why my voice was failing. After a couple of misdiagnoses, in early 2016, we all finally guessed it was some version of bulbar onset ALS. When people are as far along on the bulbar journey as I am, most can no longer eat by mouth. I feel lucky that I still can. However, not only is it getting harder to do that, but it is also taking more time. When it's as hard to eat by mouth as it is, there is a significant risk of choking or aspirating food into my lungs. But even with the associated risks, I'll keep doing it because tasting food is one of the things we humans get pleasure from. Plus, I can't help noticing when people living with ALS (Pals) start depending on a feeding tube for nourishment, they seem to give up on life. So, even with the risk of choking to death or ending up with pneumonia from aspirating food, I think it's worth it.

I also depend on more and more help from my wife, Connie. Even feeding our dog, Bella, is now a task that wears me out. I'm still able to make my hot cereal in the mornings, but by the time I make it and then eat it, an hour to an hour and a half has passed. Connie now has to make all my other meals, wash my clothes, change my bed, do the maintenance on my ventilator, and what bugs me the most, all the routine house maintenance I used to do.

I miss not being able to walk more than not talking. It helps that I have a fantastic power wheelchair that can take me on many of the trails in our small town. Getting outside every day is one of the keys to staying upbeat. But, how much longer will I be able to transfer from my manual wheelchair into the powerchair? I seem to be at the limit of my ability to do that, just as I'm nearing my ability to independently get in and out of bed. Or on or off the toilet on my own. Or in and out of the shower. Even getting dressed is now a major task that takes me about a half hour every day.

Going back to my ability to shower, it has become such a major ordeal that I only shower every other day. As I got out of bed this morning, I looked at the clock, By the time I showered and dressed, over an hour had passed. And showering and dressing are exhausting.

Speaking of the shower, little could I have imagined that my sailing, climbing, caving, and vertical rope rescue training would help in my current situation. But it has. I'm now designing and, with the help of my grandson, Blake, will build a ceiling hoist to get me in and out of the shower. And Connie is making a chest harness to lift me in and out of the shower. If all goes as planned, Connie, who weighs a hundred pounds less than I do, should be able to hoist me in and out of the shower easily. (In a month or so, I'll let you know if my idea worked.)

It was a little over a year ago that I noticed my hands were losing dexterity. This year, they have gotten worse, but I'm still able to type. Grabbing a single piece of paper out of a stack are now impossible, and writing is nearly impossible.

Because of poor circulation in my legs, my feet are always purple, usually swollen, and almost always cold. And some of my toes are starting to curl under, and because of that curling, I now have a blister on the side of a toe that isn't healing. I've been checking it each day to be sure it isn't getting infected, and so far, it's not.

I'm relatively sure respiratory failure is what will do me in. I should be using my noninvasive ventilator more than I do, but I don't particularly appreciate how it ties me down. The Trilogy ventilator is portable, but the humidifier for it isn't. And when I use it without the humidifier, my nose dries out, and I get nose bleeds.

I mentioned that the one thing that is becoming more and more clear to me is how wretched ALS is. Not only do I notice what a cruel disease it is in my case, but more importantly, I see through social media what it's doing or has done to others. I cried last night as I read a post by a young mother who has been having an extra hard time. I hesitate to say she is at the point that she is giving up, but from her post, she has now accepted that the ALS Monster will win soon. I also saw that a twenty-six-year-old man lost his battle the other day. And there was the death of a forty-something-year-old fireman I had corresponded with a few times. When he died, he left a wife and a couple of teenagers. For some reason, his death hit me harder than most, and I cried harder and longer over his death than I have the few dozen others that I've seen on Facebook.

Oh, and about my eyes. Both eyes experience fasciculations, which is just a fancy word for twitching. When I get a little stressed, both eyes have fasciculations bad enough that when I try to sleep, the eyelids flicker open and closed rapidly. The fasciculations make it impossible to sleep. So, I try not to get stressed, which is easier said than done. My eyelids also droop, making it hard to read or even see straight. When I wake up in the mornings, I often must pry my eyes open, as the orbital muscles appear to be weakening. Because of my age and the weakening orbital muscles, we are looking into blepharoplasty surgery. If I have the operation, the surgeon will remove some of the excess skin on my eyelids in hopes that I'll be able to open them wider. Over the next month, I have a couple more doctor's appointments to explore whether the surgery is worth it. I was joking with Dr. Hunter, my primary care physician, saying he'd have to refer me to Hollywood for facelift surgery. Instead, he referred me to a doctor who comes once a month to our local hospital. Per Google, her primary practice is in a suburb of Los Angeles, not all that far from Hollywood. So I may soon look younger, even though I told the doctors that I just want to be able to see better. I could care less about my looks; I just want to be able to see and read.

Yes, ALS is a hideous, wretched disease, however, I still feel lucky to be alive. I feel much more fortunate than many others I see on the ALS support group sites. I often think about how unfair it is when young people who are just starting families get hit by ALS. Or I think of the ten-year-old girl who lives near Seattle who has ALS. Shouldn't every girl who is ten be outside playing with her friends, running, jumping, and riding a bike? How could I ever feel sorry for myself, even if I do have a wretched disease like ALS when I have a wonderful wife, a beautiful home, no major financial worries, and live in a wonderful town?

May 2019. Connie is changing the drain under my handicap-accessible sink.

June 2019. Connie is adding a trickle charger to the battery in our van that has been modified to accommodate an electric wheelchair.

Better Than a Sharp Stick in the Eye

9 July 2019

The one given with ALS is that there will always be more and more declining of body functions. As expected, this is true for me, too.

When I was going through the process of being diagnosed with ALS, the neurologist kept saying that they were ruling everything else out, because as he said, "Nothing is worse than ALS." I have to disagree.

Early in 2014, I started noticing that I was losing my voice. At first it was so subtle that even my wife, Connie, didn't notice it for several months. But by August 2014, it was apparent that something was wrong, and that started us down the long road of trying to figure out the cause. By February of 2015, the first neurologist I saw diagnosed primary progressive aphasia (PPA). When the doctor told me she thought I might have PPA, she had tears in her eyes because she knew she was giving me devastating news. In February of 2016, when the doctors were starting to say ALS, both Connie and I could truthfully say, "Better than primary progressive aphasia." Crazy as it sounds, we were happy when the doctors said I had some form of bulbar ALS.

The other day a fellow pALS sent me a text and said nothing is worse than ALS. I beg to differ, knowing about PPA. I also disagree most every day of the week when I read the daily news. A few months back, there was an awful photo of a little starving girl in Yemen all over the Internet. I knew right then that I'd take ALS a hundred times over than to be that poor girl's father. Just a couple of weeks ago, there was the extra sad photo of the migrant father whose daughter drowned while trying to swim the Rio Grande river. Again, I'd take ALS over what that father went through.

Saturday morning, I woke up to a lovely message on Messenger from a woman who had just finished reading my book, *Just Another Adventure: Living with Amyotrophic Lateral Sclerosis*. Besides telling me she liked reading my book, she told me that she had lost her husband to ALS two years ago, just six months after his diagnosis. So, I say to myself, "Better than his ALS," meaning that even another individual's ALS can be worse than mine.

I might even say, "Better than a sharp stick in the eye." At least I can see. If I had to choose, I might take ALS over going blind? And I can easily say, "Better than starving." Or "Better than living in the middle of a war zone." When I look back through history, I could list a million "Better than's." "Better than the Bataan Death March." Or, "Better than five years in the Hanoi Hilton." Many people are worse off than me, and things could always be worse. ALS sucks, but life is still good.

When a Baby's First Word Is Fuck

17 July 2019

My sister-in-law, Carol, sent me a text in early May telling me that my brother Jay, ten years my senior, might have ALS. That sparked many questions and emotions. Like me, my brother is confined to a wheelchair. Jay has been suffering from COPD for the last four years, and about two years ago he started having problems walking. About a year ago he could no longer walk, and his doctors thought his loss of walking might be due to Parkinson's disease. In May, they changed their diagnoses to MS or ALS.

One of my Facebook friends recently had a post about poor punctuation and how it bugs him. I know he was mostly joshing, but I couldn't help thinking about how poor I am at punctuation and proper sentence structure. My excuse may be because I missed so much school, or was I too preoccupied with other thoughts to pay attention. Did you ever try sitting still in grade school, when the night before your stepmother had crammed the handle of a toilet plunger up your anus and you're bleeding from your rectum? Or you were forced to work into the wee hours painting interior walls of the home where you lived? Or you stayed up half the night with your older sister helping her take care of your step-siblings? Or you woke up to another beating because you fell asleep without changing a diaper of one of those step-siblings?

So, what happened to Chris? He committed suicide. To this day, I ask facetiously, "Humm. I wonder why?" I have little question about why I have no use for my father or my stepmother. Or why I felt joy when my father died. I can only imagine how good I'm going to feel when I hear Mary has passed on. Hell, I might even have a drink in celebration. And I'm not a drinker. Maybe I'll inject a shot of some good stuff directly into my PEG feeding tube.

Daily, I silently thank my older brother Fred for saving my younger sister Chelly, my older sister Andree, and me from having to spend our entire childhoods in the hell we endured for seven years. Had he not saved us, I doubt that I would have survived. I might have spent my adulthood in prison. Indeed, I would have killed Mary, or she would have killed me. In my mind, there is no doubt of that.

More than once, I have read that survivors of the Holocaust and soldiers who have witnessed the horrors of war do better mentally if they confront their past head-on. Soldiers with PTSD do better if they don't keep it bottled up inside. I guess that's what I'm doing. ALS has robbed me of my ability to talk, so I have to express my feelings in the written word. My writing is therapy to heal ancient mental wounds that never seemed to heal properly.

Even after close to 50 years, I still have nightmares about my childhood with Mary and my father. One of my recurring nightmares comes from a real experience of being woken up by being hit on the head with a hairbrush. I must have had this nightmare at least a hundred times, but it still finds a way of sneaking into my dreams. When I have that dream now, I wonder if all the head trauma I suffered at Mary's hands could be the cause of my ALS?

I could do much better with my punctuation, but I feel like I broke through enough barriers not to worry about the little things in life, like doing everything correctly when it comes to the three-Rs. I beat the odds by not following in my father's footsteps, and that's good enough for me.

You Can Call Me Hollywood

16 August 2019

When many of us think of people who have facelifts, we think of Hollywood movie stars. I'm about as far from a movie star as one can get. So why did I have a facelift? Technically it was an eyebrow lift, and the simple answer is to see better. I could care less what I look like; I just want to be able to see.

ALS has already taken away my ability to talk and walk. It has even weakened my ability to breathe and is robbing me of the use of my hands. The thought of losing one more thing was depressing. More than depressing, it was scary.

As I always do before an office visit with Dr. Hunter, my primary care physician, I print a list of my concerns. Near the end of April of this year one of my concerns was that I was experiencing endless fasciculations in my left eyebrow and eyelid. It was especially bad when I got up in the morning and as I got drowsy. When my left eyelid partially covered my eye it made it hard to see. I had researched this problem, and on one of the Facebook ALS support site asked if anyone else was having the same problem. Not surprisingly, a few people with bulbar ALS reported they were. Then, a lovely nurse from Australia told me that the procedure to fix the problem is known as a blepharoplasty, where excess skin is cut from the eyelid. Armed with the little knowledge that I had about the blepharoplasty procedure, I asked Dr. Hunter what he recommended. Since traveling is getting hard for me, he suggested that I see Dr. Mathur, the traveling ear, nose, and throat (ENT) doctor who comes to Sitka every month. Dr. Hunter told me that if anyone could help me locally, it would be Dr. Mathur, and made the referral.

In June, we met Dr. Mathur, I already knew we'd be seeing a woman doctor, which frankly made me happy. If I've learned anything about doctors over the last five years, women doctors tend to be more compassionate. Those I've met have been excellent doctors, possibly because they still must prove themselves in a male-dominated world.

What surprised me when we met her is that she is from India. Her heritage once again strengthened my belief that diversity is a good thing in our country's medical field. Within seconds of meeting her, Connie and I both liked her. One thing I especially like in any doctor is when they say, "I don't know," or say they haven't done something before. Dr. Mathur told us that she had only done one blepharoplasty during her residency, which had been a few years ago. She added that she would be willing to do the procedure, but first, wanted to talk to a colleague who is a plastic surgeon. I loved hearing that from her. I like doctors who are willing to go the extra mile. She then took several photos of my eyes and asked me to email her some pictures of my eyes when I was tired.

In July, Dr. Mathur told us that her colleague suggested that a brow lift. She said she had never done a brow lift, but felt she had the skills to do one. She then suggested that we go home, tape my eyebrows up, and see if that improved my vision. If that helped, she told us she was willing if we were.

The next morning right after breakfast, Connie taped my eyebrows to my forehead, laughing as she did it. After my eyes adjusted to the additional light, I could, indeed, see better. When Connie showed me photos with the tape, I too had to laugh. After an hour or so with the tapes in place, I emailed Dr. Mathur that we'd like to go ahead with the procedure if she was still willing.

Adding to my decision to have the procedure locally with a doctor I had full confidence in, was that the Sitka Community Hospital closed at the end of July. As is the case across America, small, rural hospitals are closing, partly because they cost too much to operate, and partly because they can't keep good doctors on staff. The Sitka Community Hospital was a victim of both circumstances. Fortunately, the local, regional Native health organization, known as Southeast Alaska Regional Health Consortium, or SEARCH, filled the void for our little town. Despite SEARCH management saying the SEARCH Hospital will not close, we know of a push to move the regional hospital to Juneau, a larger town. So, I figured that the more medical procedures we could do locally would help their bottom line. And it might not only keep them in Sitka but give them more of an incentive to build a new hospital here.

There is a high probability that the brow lift Dr. Mathur did on me is the first time one has been done in Sitka. And a unique challenge of practicing rural medicine is one of the things that keeps doctors, like Dr. Mathur coming here. With her talent, she could practice medicine anywhere she wanted.

On Wednesday, August the 14th, we went in for my pre-op visit. Dr. Mathur wanted to make sure I was still up for the brow lift, and she tried to explain to us what she would be doing. After she did some drawing on my face that made us all chuckle, we had a few questions for her. Could I use the Trilogy, my noninvasive ventilator (NIV), during the procedure? I was concerned that if I was laid flat, Iwould have a hard time breathing. I also asked if I could take a sedative to help me relax during the procedure. We were told, "no" on the sedative because the last thing they wanted was something that would relax my diaphragm muscle, compromising my breathing. But, "yes," I would be able to use the Trilogy.

Thursday the 15th quickly rolled around, and I was showered and dressed by 7:00. We arrived at the SEARCH Hospital by 7:45 for an 8:00 am check-in. After checking in, we went to the 2nd floor, and within a minute of exiting the elevator, a very friendly male nurse was ushering us to a room where I was told to take off my shoes and shirt and then to put on one of those crazy open-backed hospital gowns. Then two additional male nurses helped me transfer to the gurney with the back raised like a chair-back. The first nurse then started an IV in my right hand and said he was giving me a drug that would stop stomach acid production. [I think it also stopped my whole digestion system because about an hour after we got home, I had to pee every hour for the next 24 hours. Since I hadn't drunk or eaten anything for the previous fifteen to sixteen hours, they must have given me a liter or two of fluid via the IV. I've gotten ahead of myself, so I'll go back.]

Shortly after the IV was started, Dr. Mathur, smiling and obviously happy, came into the room. She wanted to draw the lines in a purple pen where she'd be cutting too on my forehead. When she stepped out for a minute, Connie, laughing, said, "You look like a drag queen." That made me laugh and removed a little of my anxiety.

Upon returning Dr. Mathur asked to see the Trilogy. Connie showed her and said that she had already shown Laura, one of the nurses who would be in the operating room, how to operate it. Kim, the respiratory specialist, came into the room, and after a short discussion, they decided, to my great relief, that I could use the Trilogy NIV during the procedure. I knew I'd feel better with some help breathing and was far less likely to panic.

A few minutes later when Dr. Mathur walked out of the room, she turned and said, "See you in my playground." That, too, made me feel more relaxed;. it meant that she was enjoying her work. If you enjoy your work, you will do a better job. Seeing Dr. Mathur in a good mood, about to perform a procedure she'd never done, made me recall times I had done new things in my working career. Like her, I always got excited when doing something new and creative. When I embarked on the journey of new endeavors, I felt happy, knowing that I'd be using the skills I had built up over the years to make something of beauty. I thought about a Monet bridge that I'd been asked to design and build just as I was starting to show signs of ALS. I'm darn proud of how that bridge turned out, and knew that Dr. Mathur would be able to look back with pride on what she did to improve my vision.

There was a noticeable difference in the hospital's surgical wing temperature. I was already a little chilly, so by the time they wheeled me past what they called "the beach chair," I was starting to shiver. Dr. Mathur thought it would be just as easy to do the procedure with me sitting on the gurney so, they started to get me ready and offered me a special blanket that looks like an air mattress that they blow hot air into. More chilled, I happily shook my head "yes." They put another blanket over me, and ,after I put on the Trilogy mask, covered all my head except my eyes. One of the ladies put a plastic sheet with sticky tape on one side under my eyes, and said it looked like I was wearing a burka, which made me chuckle. And after washing the exposed part of my face with what I assume was a Betadine, another lady said, "You look like an orange-faced person wearing a burka." That, too, made me laugh, especially in combination with Connie's drag queen comment. So, there I was, an orange-faced drag queen, wearing a burka, about to get a facelift. I'm sure I laughed loud enough that everyone heard me.

It was about then that I think Dr. Mathur said, "Let's take a timeout." She said my name, what I was there for, and what everyone's job would be. She told all of us how much local anesthetic she had mixed, how much she planned to use, and how much reserve she figured she had. The local anesthetic was a mixture of lidocaine and some other drug that I missed. Shortly after, she told me to be ready for a poke that she said would burn for a while. I hardly felt the jab, and the burning was so minor that it was hardly worth mention. But since I have always hated needles, I appreciated the warning.

After the local anesthetic kicked in, I felt the sensation of Dr. Mathur cutting above my left eyebrow. I could hear everything that was being said, and I could also hear a suction noise, much like in a dental office. I assumed that was blood from the incision being sucked up. Dr. Mathur would, from time to time, ask for a four by four, which I deduced was a four-inch square piece of gauze. I could then feel her dabbing that gauze on the forehead. She then warned me that I might smell some burning flesh from the cauterization of the incision. Because the Trilogy was feeding me air, I didn't smell anything, but I sure felt it. It wasn't painful, but I still jumped in surprise because I could feel an electric shock. With each cauterization buzz, I could first feel what can best be described as a static electric shock with the hair on my head standing straight up —then building to the point that I could feel the electricity flow through my body all the way to the grounding pad they had earlier placed on my right calf. I knew the shock wouldn't kill me, but I didn't enjoy that part of the procedure - not one bit. However, I also laughed to myself, remembering something that had happened to me way back when I was around twenty and working as an apprentice machinist. In my mind's eye, I could see myself standing behind an old metal lathe turning a long steel shaft. Sometimes, the metal shavings came off the carbide tool in a long endless-flowing metal strand. Not only is this a nuisance, but it can be dangerous. Even knowing better, I grabbed the razor-sharp streaming chip, and as I pulled back on it, I received one of the most unusual injuries of my life. Not only did the metal strand cut all the fingers on my right hand to the bone, but the hot chip also burnt the skin, searing the skin as it cut. And, if that wasn't enough, as I pulled the strand towards myself, I also pulled the sharp, hot streaming chip through the power cord that fed the light mounted on the lathe carriage. Within a second, I had cut my fingers, burnt them to the point that smoke was coming off the flesh, and I also gotten an electric shock for a split second until the breaker tripped. My nostalgic trip back to the '70s occupied my mind as Dr. Mathur did her magic.

In about an hour and a half Dr. Mathur had finished with my left eyebrow. And now, I was now overly hot. I could feel sweat running off my legs and chest. Since I can't talk, I had no way of telling them that I was roasting. About that time Dr. Mathur said she was also getting hot, and I was thankful Laura asked me if I was hot. We had previously worked out a hand signal. She was holding my left hand and said, "Give my hand one squeeze if you're hot and two if not." I squeezed Laura's hand maybe with a little too much enthusiasm, and, was extra glad they turned off the warm air blowing into the air mattress-type blanket. They also pulled a blanket off me, for which I was grateful. Even better, Laura put three ice packs under the blanket to cool me down. By the time they started on my right eyebrow, I felt much better.

At a little break before my right eyebrow lift, I asked to have my back in more of a reclining angle. When I reached my left arm out from the blanket and tried to signal my wishes. Dr. Mathur assumed I was trying to touch the eyebrow she had just finished, and she said in a somewhat panicked voice, "Don't touch." That's one problem of not talking. How could I use charades to communicate that my butt and back were getting very sore? I reached out away from the gurney and gave the down single that I'd use if I was directing a crane operator to lower a load. Fortunately, someone understood, and soon the back of the gurney was adjusted. She had said her back was getting sore, and the last thing I wanted was for her to be uncomfortable.

Dr. Mathur started on the right side a little after 11:00. Even though I'd been in the OR longer than I would have guessed, the time was passing quickly. Since they wouldn't give me a sedative, I had to do mind games to stay calm. Even though I had 100% confidence in Dr. Mathur and the whole team, it's not easy to remain calm when someone is cutting chunks of skin off my forehead and, sending electrical currents through my body.

In my head, I was designing a greenhouse for the same people I'd designed the Monet bridge for. I was figuring out the floor drain and how I'd make the floors and walls watertight so the greenhouse could be hosed out. Since the proposed greenhouse sits up about 12 feet off the ground to be level with the floor of the house, I had a few more problems to solve. I was remembering how I'd built the deck the greenhouse would look over, and how to make it blend in with the house, which I think is the most attractive house my company had ever built. I wanted people to look at the greenhouse and be awed by it, just like they are by the house, the Monet bridge, and the hot tub gazebo that the bridge leads to.

I hardly felt anything when Dr. Mathur cauterized the incisions on my right eyebrow. Maybe my legs had sweated and the grounding pad had better conductivity to my body? Or, possibly I was just too deep into figuring out the greenhouse design. Either way, I was a little surprised to hear Dr. Mathur say she was wrapping up. Unless I wasn't tracking the time right, she did the right eyebrow in half the time that she did the left one. She had told Connie and me that she'd be slow on the first eye and that the second one would go quicker, and I think that was the case.

Postscript: I'm writing this part in late January of 2021, and I can still see much better than I could pre-surgery. I can't definitively say if ALS or my age caused the sagging eyebrows. I can say the surgery worked, and I'm extra glad I trusted Dr. Mathur to do it.

Self-Worth

18 August 2019

Today, being a Sunday and a family day for many, must be a hard day on some when dealing with the ALS Monster. My Facebook Messenger has been dinging like crazy. Some of the messages are from relatives and some from new Facebook friends. And, I've had several people ask me how I stay positive. That is not an easy question to answer, especially when I only know a little about the person asking the question. Here's some general advice. I hope it helps. It helps me to put my thoughts into words.

Besides air, water, and food, one of the essentials for survival is to feel needed, loved, and feel like you're contributing. As ALS progresses, we lose our ability to contribute to the financial well-being of our families and lose our ability to contribute to daily tasks like preparing meals, washing dishes, and all the things we used to look at as mundane tasks. Further, we feel like we are a drain on resources as we become more and more dependent on our loved ones or caretakers. So we have to find ways we can still contribute, even if just a little. That's one of the reasons I write and have self-published one book and will soon be able to release a second. But my writing is not enough to fulfill my need to feel like I'm contributing to society. That's why I volunteer my time to others.

As a contractor and builder forced into retirement by my ALS, I was happy when asked almost five years ago to volunteer my time on a building committee to help renovate a historic building. The building is the headquarters for the Sitka Summer Music Festival, a nonprofit that my wife, Connie, and I have supported for several years. I started volunteering on the building committee as I was losing my voice and fighting the effects of acromegaly. Fortunately, after what was literally brain surgery, I won the battle with acromegaly, but as I was beating acro, my voice kept fading away. As my voice faded to nothing, I gave up a volunteer position with another nonprofit, and hoped that the Music Festival would let me stay. Not only did they let me stay, but they accommodated my special needs. For that, I owe a big thank you. I gained more from them than they have from me. As the ALS Monster took more and more from me, I still felt as if I were giving something to my community. To my great happiness, renovation work will soon start on the historic building. As the work progresses, there will be less and less need for the building committee's work. That means I'll be looking for another volunteer job I can do sitting in front of my computer.

When asked how I stay positive, my volunteer work has helped. Maybe it will for you? Spend part of your day volunteering. A public-school teacher who was forced to quit the job she loved once asked me, "What could I do?" My suggestion was volunteer to correct school papers or help with lesson plans. If she could still talk, she could read to young school kids or at a senior center. With a bit of imagination, most of us can find something a volunteer slot. I'm considering doing research and helping write letters to influence political things I support. Technology will let me Google and research nonprofits that I support. I can then write summaries for their busy board members the results of my research. No matter what your political views might be, write to your politicians. If there is a nonprofit you believe in, offer to help with their research or volunteer to write letters for them.

Volunteering is good medicine that will help you feel better about yourself. And, when you feel like you are making the world a little better, you're going to be happier. It does no good to dwell on the negatives of ALS or any disease. And lots to be gained, especially if you feel like you contribute something to your community.

A Puppy Peed on Me

21 August 2019

Yesterday, as I often do in the morning, I decided to lie down for a nap. That morning was like any other morning, except Connie had gone hiking and berry picking with Myrna. The two gals had driven up the Harbor Mountain Road, a lane and a half gravel road with lots of twists and turns. At the end of the road, there is a trail that leads into some of the most spectacular views I've ever seen, perhaps in the world. The mountains themselves are striking, but even more stunning is the view looking out to the ocean. Already close to heaven, thousands of bushes are filled with the most delicious, sweet blueberries this time of year. That's what the ladies were after.

After sleeping for around 45 minutes, I sat on the bed's edge, took off the mask that provides me air while I sleep, grabbed my glasses off the nightstand, put them on, and grabbed my iPhone. Before I laid down, I had been listening to the podcast *Hidden Brain* with Shankar Vedantam. In that episode, "Rebel with a Cause," Mr. Vedantam was interviewing human behavior scientist

Francesca Gino about how people often are successful by not following their peers' norms. As I restarted the podcast just before transferring from my bed to my manual wheelchair, the two scientists gave different examples. The one playing as I started the transfer was how airline pilot Sully Sullenberger saved the lives of 155 people through his actions of not following the rules. If you recall, Mr. Sullenberger landed the plane he was piloting in the Hudson River in 2009 after the plane's engines were disabled on takeoff when the plane hit a flock of birds. By staying calm while making split-second decisions and not needing a runway to land, Mr. Sullenberger avoided what could have been a catastrophic plane crash.

The technique I use to transfer from the bed to my wheelchair is to pull the chair close to the bed, sitting with the chair's right side facing the bed. Making sure the brakes are locked, I reach my left arm all the way over to the left armrest on the wheelchair. I then place my right arm on the bed, and with one movement, I push up my body with both arms while using the limited strength in my legs to assist. When all goes as planned, after I'm up, I pivot on my feet and sit in the chair. This time, things didn't go as planned. As I lowered myself, the right side of the chair rolled backward, and I found myself sitting on the floor. Ugh, now what? I needed to think, so I turned the podcast off.

Well, if Sully Sullenberger could save himself and a plane full of people, I should be able to get myself back up and into the chair. I laid all the way down on the floor, looked up at the wheelchair, and saw that the right-side brake was no longer locked. Sometimes before I transfer, the brake handle hits the side of the bed and unlocks. When this has happened in the past, I've still been able to get into the chair, but I wasn't lucky this time. After unlocking the other brake, I started squirming myself to the end of the bed, pulling the chair along behind me. I was hoping that if I could grab the end of the toe-board at the end of the bed, I could get into my chair. Alas, I couldn't.

After taking a breather, I figured, maybe if I belly-scooted into the bath-room, where I could brace my feet against the wall, I could pull myself up using the floor to ceiling pole next to the toilet. Pulling my wheelchair behind me, I slowly made my way into the bathroom. When I reached the pole, I got about halfway up, but it was soon apparent that it, too, was not going to work. As I slid back down the pole, I somehow knocked off my glasses, and I was afraid I'd smash them under myself. When I reached them, I set them on the vanity. By this time, I'd been on the floor close to a half-hour and I was getting pooped. I slithered a bit more until I could pull a towel off the rack and make myself a pillow. I knew I'd need help getting up.

After a short rest lying on the cold tile, I pulled my phone out of my pocket with the intent of texting or calling my son, Zach. But, with no glasses, it was hard seeing the phone. The phone-screen had switched from vertical mode to horizontal, which made texting harder for me. I managed to text to Zach's and his families' cell phones, but wasn't sure they went through. They live in an area with spotty cell service. Would anyone ever see the text? I thought about texting Connie's cell, but she, too, was in an area with spotty service. And her cell phone was probably in a backpack where she wouldn't hear the ding. And if I did get a hold of Connie, the two ladies might drive down the Harbor Mountain Road faster than they should. So, I decided to call Zach's home phone, but could I see well enough to dial it or find it in my contacts? I regret-ted putting my glasses on the vanity. It would be an epic backtrack to retrieve them.

Because Zach is at the very end of my contact list made it easier than it might have been to find his number. I hit the "Dial" command, and within a couple of rings, my grandson, Blake, answered the phone. I hoped that he saw the caller ID, and after a couple of grunts and a few taps on the wall, Blake knew something was wrong. I heard both him and his mother, Jenn, yelling for Zach. Soon Blake said, "We are on our way. We will be there soon."

One of bulbar ALS's typical symptoms is to be over-emotional, and after hearing that help was on the way, I started crying. To get my emotions under control and to kill the 15 minutes that I knew it would take for the rescue team to arrive, I turned the podcast back on. I had to face facts; I was no Sully Sullenberger.

In less than 15 minutes, I heard the rescue crew at the back door, and soon, Zach was standing over me. When he turned on the bathroom light, I found myself being attacked by an extremely cute little three-month-old border collie named Sara. As she jumped up on my face, tail wagging and tongue licking, I started to laugh. Zach reported, "She peed on the floor." I could feel my shirt sleeve getting wet, which made me laugh even more. Soon, as puppies always do, she ran off to explore new things while Zach grabbed some paper towels and cleaned up the pee.

August 21, 2019. A selfie right after I fell. You can see the discoloration around my eyes from the eyebrow lift surgery I had. My eyebrows are also covered with an ointment to enhance the healing process.

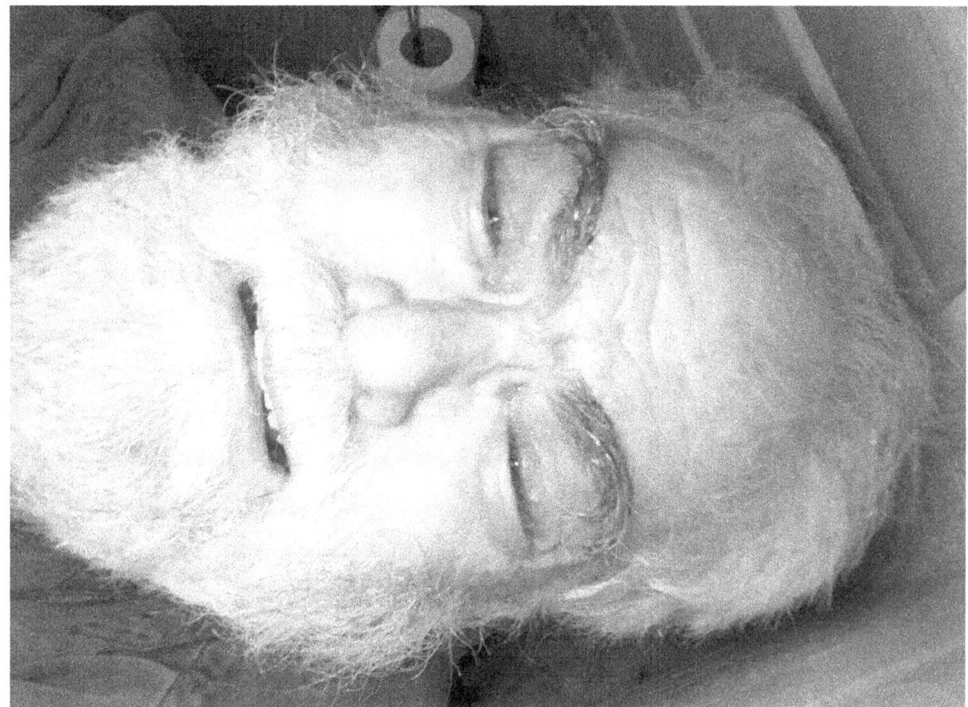

August 21, 2019. Another selfie. After I called, I got emotional and started crying.

A couple of minutes later Zach and Blake had lifted me back into my wheelchair. As I laughed both in relief over being rescued and the puppy baptism, I rolled over, grabbed my glasses, and put them on. I could then see to type into my phone and explain what happened. I thanked my family for coming to my rescue, and I assured them that I was okay. And, as I heard them head back to their day, I changed my shirt, laughing at the way a cute little dog had peed on me.

When Connie got home, we figured out how to lock the wheelchair brakes securely. There is a hole drilled in the brake handle. All it takes is a pin pushed through the hole to lock the brakes completely. We stopped at the marine hardware store on our afternoon walk and bought a pin that works perfectly. This morning, Connie rigged up a self-rescue system that we think will work if I need it in the future. We hope I don't have to test the system, but it's good knowing there's an option. More importantly, I want Connie not to feel like

August 21, 2019. Sara enjoys a rawhide chew after she peed on me.

she has to be at home 24/7. She deserves a life, and I don't want to burden her any more than I already do.

ALS sucks, but life is good. Life is even better when dogs and puppies are involved, even if the puppy pees on you.

Revisionist History

24 August 2019

I'm a big fan of Malcolm Gladwell, and I especially like his podcast, *Revisionist History*. In that podcast, Mr. Gladwell explores various topics, from music to sports, medicine, and many others. He digs deep into each subject and then unravels misunderstood or misleading concepts. In one of his in-depth investigations from four years ago, he investigated the hysteria about the runaway vehicles that led to several fatal crashes. Several automobile manufacturers recalled millions of cars worldwide to fix a perceived problem. Toyota ended up paying out over a billion dollars in damages. In the podcast entitled *Blame Game*, Mr. Gladwell, reported how test after test proved that even the most powerful engines couldn't overpower properly functioning brakes, if the accelerator was pushed to the floor. So, did hysteria overrule common sense? It seems that way. The tests showed a more likely scenario: Panicked drivers, thinking they were pressing on the brakes, were, in fact, pressing on the accelerator. Several computer readouts from the crashed cars confirmed this to be so, but the press fueled the hysteria overruling the facts.

In the episode I listened to today, entitled "The Obscure Virus Club," Mr. Gladwell talks about a group of scientists who specialized in virology. The scientists were ridiculed when they dared to suggest that certain types of viruses can alter DNA and cause diseases, including cancers in animals. When the scientists presented their research, several prestigious scientific publications refused to publish their findings and called them lunatics. In the end, the scientists were right. Their research proved that a retrovirus could indeed alter DNA. In fact, in 1975, three of them, David Baltimore, Howard Temin, and Renato Dulbecco, shared a Nobel Prize for Medicine for their groundbreaking work that others had discredited. Their pioneering work led others to discover the role that a retrovirus plays in AIDS to take their discovery further. Without the work done by the Obscure Virus Club, the AIDS epidemic likely would have been much worse than it was.

Many discoveries prove that thinking out of the box that leads to significant breakthroughs in every scientific field. Another example is the long-held belief that the Americas were peopled via the Bering Land Bridge. As a non-scientist observer, I have personally known people who have been ridiculed for suggesting that boats might have played a role in human migration to the Americas. Yet, when you look at the history of glaciation, one can easily challenge the Bering Land Bridge theory. I cringe each time I hear the old school teachings of the land bridge. I want to scream, "Look at the evidence before you close the door on other theories."

In the podcast I listened to today, David Baltimore said something that made me think of ALS. The jist of what he said was, "If you don't understand the cause of a disease, that leads to fantasies." I think that means we must understand how a disease starts before we have much hope of finding a cure. With ALS, we know that the motor neurons stop functioning correctly, leading to the brain's failure to communicate with the body's muscles properly. However, with sporadic ALS, we still have no idea why one's motor neurons quit working. That's why if a cure is to be found, we need to separate the fantasies from reality. Possibly, we need to start listening to some of the scientists that are being discounted as lunatics. Just like retroviruses were dismissed as impossible, we now know that they exist. We also know that retroviruses can change DNA. Could it be a virus or a combination of viruses that sparks the decline of motor neurons? I don't have any idea. However, conventional thinking hasn't made much progress in finding a cure for ALS. Is it time to expand the out-of-the-box thinking to make progress with ALS research? Again, I don't know. There is an excellent chance, though, that some unknown scientist in some unknown lab might be on the brink of discovering the cause of sporadic ALS. Let's hope for minds open to ideas that might seem farfetched. It's human nature to get so entrenched in one's views that any idea that challenges a long-held belief is automatically discounted. We can all learn a valuable lesson from the Obscure Virus Club.

Living on the Edge

9 September 2019

I've always liked living on the edge, possibly too close to the edge. So it will not come as a surprise to many that I came within a hair's breadth of going over that edge today.

Sundays are the day we spend with our three grandsons. Since the weather was beautiful, we decided to go for a stroll and roll; everyone walks while I roll along in my power wheelchair. I suggested that we go to a new trail that I'd had only taken a wheelchair on once before. There were a few very steep hills, but if I hit them at full speed, I could get up them. And, even if I couldn't, the boys have pushed me up steep hills in the past. So, off we went.

As we parked the van, Connie commented that the last time we had gone on this trail, it had scared her nearly to death. After rolling out of the van, I took off up the first hills. At the top on a flat place, I could see 13-year-old Nate and his 17-year-old brother Blake right behind me. Blake then asked, "Do you come here often?" I shook my head, "No," and started up the last hill.

After getting to the top of that hill, I waited again, then tilted my chair back a bit to go down a very steep and long hill. This was the hill that had scared Connie the first time we'd been on the trail, and if truth be told, it scared me a bit too. I estimate it averaged over 30 degrees down-sloping, with that last twenty feet being close to 40 degrees.

Since I'd been down the hill once, and since this is a loop trail, I wouldn't have to come back up it, so I slowly started down. I could hear Blake and Nate talking right behind me. As I hit the steepest part of the trail, my wheelchair started what is called a pitchpole in the sailing world; the chair began to do an ass- over-teakettle roll. I felt the rear wheels lift off the ground and felt my ankles bending as the footrest hit the ground. I instinctively put my hands out, and just as I felt gravel on my hands, the two boys grabbed the chair. Fear of my head hitting the ground and then a 405-pound wheelchair rolling over me gave me enough distraction that I couldn't hear their panicked words. I also wondered if the seatbelt I always wear was a good idea.Without it, maybe I'd get lucky, do a face plant, and the chair would roll to the side. But I was strapped in.

As the saying goes, "I saw my life flashing in front of my eyes." In less than ten seconds after the pitchpole started, Blake and Nate had arrested the roll. I soon felt my hands lifting off the ground, but I also felt myself sliding further forward. My additional weight moving forward would make it harder for the boys to roll me back onto all four wheels. Fortunately, Connie came running, and the two boys, along with their grandmother, soon had me back upright. As the boys held the back of my chair, I rolled on down to the bottom of the hill. We were all a little shaken. I could have been badly hurt, but I had once again escaped with nothing more than sore ankles.

When we reached the sidewalk at the end of the gravel trail, the boys, my wife, and our dog huddled around. I typed into my phone, "Thank you for saving me. It was my fault for not having the chair tipped back far enough." To which 9-year-old Dane said, "We all learn from our mistakes." I responded, "Yes, I learned never to take that trail again." And rest assured, I won't, not that Connie would ever let me. Maybe, today was payback for the three times in our long marriage when Connie was living too close to the edge, and I watched her nearly fall to her death. I just hope Connie doesn't experience the nightmares I've had at watching her close brushes with death.

You'd think that ALS might stop me from taking crazy risks, but life is always risky, and living requires us all to take them. MaybeI push things a little further than I should? Nah, life isn't worth living if you don't stick your toe in the water from time to time. As I type this, I'm as happy as I can be, so maybe another close call was just what the doctor ordered. I'm also pleased knowing my grandsons saved my bacon today. Thanks, guys.

Visiting Neurologist

30 October 2019

Today I saw a visiting neurologist, the first neurologist I've seen in over a year and a half. When our small-town hospital shut down at the end of July and was purchased by Southeast Alaska Regional Health Consortium (SEARHC), the regional Native Health Hospital, we were worried that we'd have fewer health-care options. Our worries seemed to be unfounded. SEARHC has added several visiting specialists to their schedule, and one of the specialties is a neurologist. Ends up, the doctor I saw today has recently retired after a long career at Swedish Hospital in Seattle. He said, as a new experience, he will be coming to Sitka every three months.

There isn't much any doctor, even a neurologist, can do for me when it comes to ALS, it's also nice to be seen by a doctor with many years of experience working with ALS patients. Even better, his boss at Swedish Hospital in Seattle was one of the most respected ALS specialists in the Northwest and is the doctor who diagnosed my ALS. So the doctor I saw today said he'd be talking to his former boss about my case and history.

There is a big positive take-away from today's visit. To paraphrase his words, "You know you're beating the odds. bulbar ALS is often very aggressive, and it's nearly six years since your first symptoms. That's twice the expected life expectancy of three years." He continued, "I came in early this morning to read over the files of the patients I'd be seeing today. When I read yours, one of the things I kept reading in your file is that all the doctors say you are always amiable and have a good attitude. A good attitude goes a long way to helping with longevity."

I hate going to the doctor. But today was an exception, and I'm looking forward to seeing him again in three months. After that visit, I'll likely plan on seeing him every six months.

ALS sucks, but life is good, and it's good to know that even in our remote little Alaskan town, we have access to excellent healthcare without having to travel out of town.

Runaway Dream

1 November 2019

The other day, even after a good night's sleep, I was still tired, so I took a morning nap. That's something I've been doing more and more of lately. And I've been relying on an after-lunch nap to get me through 'til bedtime. The morning nap didn't do the trick, so after I ate lunch, it was right back to bed for me. And wow, did I sleep hard, hard enough that I fell right asleep and didn't hear Connie leave when she and Bella went for their afternoon walk.

I have no idea how long the dream was, but it seemed to go on and on. Or should I have said nightmare? I dreamt that I was riding around in an extensive library in my 405-pound wheelchair. I was cruising up and down the aisles looking at books when all of a sudden, my controls wouldn't work. I'd pull the joystick to go right, and the chair would go left. I kept crashing into the shelving, and I left piles of books in my wake as I careened off one bookshelf after another. I'd try to back up, and the chair would speed ahead.When I reached down for the On/Off switch, it broke off in my hands. I finally made it into a large area where many people were standing around watching me and my out-of-control wheelchair. If I could only talk, I'd tell them where the breaker was for the battery. Since I couldn't, I kept pointing behind the chair, hoping that someone would get the hint that I wanted them to turn off the breaker that sits low on the back of the battery pack. Funny, I saw Jimmy, my childhood friend, and I knew if anyone understood, my hand gestures, it would be him. And, sure enough, he understood. But he said, "No can do. If I got down that low, I'd never be able to get back up. Sorry." So, the chair just kept going around and around in circles.

Knowing I had recently changed the battery, I wondered how long it would last. Doing some math in my head, I figured the battery would last a few hours. Ugh, what was I to do? At long last, I got the chair to head in a straight line, and I crashed into a wall, crushing my feet in the process. The wheels spun, and started smoking as the friction burnt the carpet. Would that friction start a fire? More critical, why was no one helping me? My feet kept hurting, and as I looked down, I could see there was blood pouring out of my slippers. With a lot of pulling on the joystick, I backed the chair back. Maybe, if I got the chair outside, I could somehow maneuver it into a safe place to let the battery run down? Heading for the exit, I found I needed to go down a very long set of stairs. I thought to myself, this is going to hurt, and hurt bad. I again pulled the joystick back, stopping just as the wheelchair's wheels started to go over the edge. I was saved just in time, but now what?

I found myself back in the same room, still full of people who neither seemed to see my problem, nor didn't care. Worse, instead of slowing down, the chair was now going faster and faster. I kept pulling back on the switch, but the chair, instead of slowing down, sped up. As I wound around and around, bouncing off walls and bookshelves, I saw a young boy crawling out of a doorway. I was now terrified that I was going to hit him. The joystick still wasn't responding, and if that wasn't bad enough, it broke off in my hands. The toddler was getting closer with each circling of the chair; I was just inches from running him over. Where were his parents? Why was no one saving him or me? With no working controls, I jumped out of the chair. As the chair ran over me, it tipped on its side and I was able to flip the breaker to Off.

I awoke to find myself half-awake and half-asleep. For a few minutes, I laid in bed trying to sort out the reality from the dream. As I gained consciousness, I realized that for some time I've been wondering what would happen if the joystick or other controls stopped working. Would I crash into someone? Would I go off a curb and tip the chair over? I can't answer those questions. If I do ever experience problems, I hope my dream doesn't come true in any shape or form.

Dirtbag Diaries

By Connie LaPerriere –– A submission to the *Dirtbag Diaries* podcast.

2 November2019

It was the first cave we'd rappelled into. After surveying, and mapping about a hundred feet of horizontal passage, we were about to do our first rappel within the cave, and my husband, Marcel, was stuck while hanging on the rope. He could not go up or down. The vertical passage was tight and too tight for anyone else to be much help. He had to find a way out by himself.

Finding a way out by himself was not new to him. He left home at fourteen because of his abusive parents. He has been a climber, and he'd had mountains throw storms, cold, and scaling problems at him. He had learned from the experiences and survived. The difference this time was that I was with him.

We hadn't meant to become cavers. It was an accident. Our son had signed up for a caving meeting and then left town. We went instead and were hooked by the intrigue of exploring the unknown. After that, we had practiced rope work since the caves in Southeast Alaska are almost all vertical. Unlike climbing, cavers often have to use the rope to go up and down wet and slimy cave walls. We learned how to survey and map caves. Then came the highly anticipated first day of caving. Thirty minutes into the cave, we rigged the rope, and off he went. The configuration of the cave and the rigging caused the rope to pull him into a vertical slot where he got severely stuck.

We threw him a line. It didn't help, and I was getting worried. All cavers have the specter of Floyd Collins's death in the back of our minds. Although this was a different situation from the tight crack Floyd had been stuck and died in, we also knew about suspension trauma. This syndrome occurs when you hang free in a harness—hanging free causes the blood to pool in your legs and becomes a cardio problem that results in death. This can happen rapidly. At least he was still moving and struggling to free himself. I was also worried about hypothermia. The caves in Southeast Alaska are wet, cold, and often have a wind blowing within them. I was getting cold waiting for him to get free. At least I was in a position to move around freely to get warm. Marcel kept trying different things before at last, he wriggled free.

After he changed the rigging on the rope, the drop was no problem for any of us. It had taken so long to free himself that we were done for the day. This was not the start I had pictured for our caving trip. Still, the next day, we returned, and down we all went. Another lesson: rigging matters. Before I knew it, we were crawling on our bellies, surveying the virgin passage, and having fun. We saw the geology of the Mesozoic limestone walls full of polished brachiopods from the spiraling flow of water. What fun to crawl inside the plumbing of the cave. What a privilege. We were hooked.

We would have many other caving adventures. Marcel carried his love of adventure and went on to become a cave diver. Then, Marcel, along with his partners, Alan Murray, and Craig Sempert, were the first divers to dive within a couple of the Southeast Alaskan caves.

Marcel LaPerriere

Marcel's first time getting stuck wasn't his last time. Another time he was in a saltwater cave. His diving partner could see he was stuck but realized that anything he did would make the situation worse, so he stayed by and waited. First, my husband snagged his weight belt, and it fell off. Then he knocked the mask up onto his forehead and pulled the regulator most of the way out of his mouth. He was breathing half saltwater and couldn't see, but at least he was making progress. He knew that panic kills. He also knew that it is impossible to panic if your breathing is under control. I guess it was not easy to control panic when breathing half saltwater. I sure couldn't have stayed calm enough if I was sipping air between gulps of water. But somehow, Marcel did.

At last, he wriggled free. Then his dive partner, Alan, could help him get the gear repositioned. They could then swim to the surface safely and call it a day, knowing it had been a very close call.

Now Marcel is facing his greatest challenge. He has amyotrophic lateral sclerosis, ALS. This is much the same as his other challenges in that death is on the line. Perhaps because of the adventures and brushes with death, we understand more than most that the difference between life and death is a very fine line. He has looked at this disease in the eye and found how to deal with it with grace and with the same kind of problem-solving abilities he has always used. Sure, it is frustrating, as were many of our other adventures. But accepting defeat and giving up has never been an option for him.

My name is Connie LaPerriere, and I submitted this short because ALS has robbed my husband of his ability to talk. However, he has not lost his spirit.

March 1994. Marcel was exiting the water while Alan Murray prepares to exit the water in the sinkhole. The pair had just completed a dive to over 260 feet in Diepolder Cave in Florida. Photo courtesy of Mary Kowalewski.

Veteran's Day

11 November 2019

In some ways, this essay doesn't fit within a book about living with ALS. However, since ALS is twice as likely to occur in military veterans as the general population, maybe it is fitting. I have many veterans in my family, from my father, brother Fred, and his wife Kay, but perhaps the most heroic of them was my father-in-law, George Durkop. That's why on this day, when we honor all vets, I felt an urge to write about a man whom I deeply respected and liked.

Veterans Day is a day that we pay our respect to the many brave men and women who have given so much for us over the last two centuries. I find it a tad hard to be patriotic in today's world. A world where we seem to no longer live up to the high standards that many of those brave veterans gave their lives for. When nearly half of the American citizens stand behind a leader who praises dictators, insults and abandons allies, and does little to quell white supremacists or other hate groups, my patriotism wanes.

1944. George, his brother Thoralf, Jr. (Bud,) his father Thoralf, and brother John before the sinking of the Gambier Bay.

But when I recall all my father-in-law, George Durkop, gave to the USA and the high standard that he lived, I cannot help but feel pride. I'm not only proud of my wife's father, but am proud of what he and so many others from his generation stood for.

George served active duty in three wars: the Second World War, Korea, and Vietnam.

During WWII, he was stationed aboard the aircraft carrier USS Gambier Bay on the fateful day of October 25th, 1944, when the aircraft carrier was sunk. During the Leyte Gulf Naval Battle, George served as Gunner's Mate 3/C when the ship was hit by several 8" shells fired by the Japanese war ship HI-JMS Chikuma and at least two other Japanese ships. Before being rescued, he spent over two days swimming in the ocean, for which he earned his first Pur-

TUESDAY, DECEMBER 12, 1944

DENVER SAILOR GLAD SHARKS DIDN'T GET HIS SUNBURNED FEET

Sunburned feet are part of the price a sailor pays for having his flat-top shot from under him, but they're far better than shark bites, George Durkop, 19, son of Patrolman and Mrs. T. A. Durkop of 3294 Newton street, discovered recently off the Philippines. Young Durkop, a gunner's mate third class, which he says is the equivalent of "buck sergeant" in the army, was a member of an anti-aircraft gun crew aboard one of the small carriers sunk by Jap naval gunfire in the sea action supporting the landings on Leyte. Forced to go overboard and swim for his life, he and several fellow crew members clung to a floater net for two days.

George Durkop.

Their bare feet, unaccustomed to the blistering effect of the tropical sun, were burned raw. They did not dare put them under water because of sharks. Compared to that, a bit of shrapnel in one leg was a minor annoyance to Durkop.

The second night they saw land ten miles away, and the next day they were picked up by an American patrol craft, put aboard a landing-ship-tank, then transferred to a hospital ship. From Leyte, they were taken to an army hospital in New Guinea, then sent home on a transport.

Durkop arrived from San Francisco Thursday afternoon on leave. He was born here, was a senior at North high school when he enlisted in February, 1943. After boot training at Farragut, Ida., and gunnery school at Treasure Island, he went to sea, and has had eleven months' of ship duty in the Pacific. He rates the Asiatic and American theater ribbons with four Bronze Stars for major engagements.

Sailor Durkop has two army brothers, John in the Philippines, Thoralf Jr. in New Guinea. Altho he was close to both of them, during his latest voyage, he saw neither of them.

December 12, 1944. Article about George Durkop in the Denver Post.

ple Heart Medal. After a few weeks of convalescing, he was stationed on the destroyer, USS Hubbard, where he finished out the war.

At the end of the second World War, he joined the US Air Force.

During the Korean War, he served active duty. I believe he earned another Purple Heart there, but never heard how he earned that one. As far as I know, he never told anyone in his family.

In 1968, during the Pueblo Incident, the Colorado Air National Guard was called up for active duty. While the rest of his unit was sent to Vietnam, George was sent to Korea for the second time. During this duty, George and one other Air Force NCO were stationed with an Army unit near the DMZ as air-support spotters. During this hot time in the Cold War, he spent 13 months within a few miles of the DMZ.

In the 1980s, George retired as a Senior Chief Master Sergeant. At the time of his retirement, he was the highest-ranking enlisted man in the Colorado National Guard, an honor that few can claim.

George was a very humble and quiet man who seldom talked of his time in the military. Once shortly before his death, I felt honored when he recounted the full details of the Gambier Bay sinking to me. After hearing how he watched men being blown up, burned to death, and some get eaten by sharks, I could understand why he didn't like to talk about some of the darker things he had seen in his life. The day he told me about his time on the Gambier Bay was also the same day he asked me to do him a favor. George asked that Connie and I, after his death, take care of his wife, Millie. We would have anyway, but his trust once again honored me.

To me, George was a real American Hero. George, I salute your memory, and thank you for all that you gave to the USA!

Postscript: When George told me his story of being on the Gambier Bay, he and I were sitting in the living room of Connie's childhood home. Connie and her mother were in the kitchen. Connie's jaw dropped when she overheard part of what her dad was telling me; George was telling me things he never spoke of. Additionally, Connie heard for the first time that George was blown into the water. He'd always said that he'd jumped in after seeing the ship was sinking, likely to shield his daughter from the truth. What I heard, and I don't think Connie did, was a shell hit the gun he was stationed at, killing almost everyone. When the shell hit, George was in a room where ammunition was being readied for use. A few seconds after the gun was obliterated, that ammunition blew up. The explosion blew a hole in the hull, and a split-second later, George went flying through that hole. Besides a shrapnel wound to the leg, I'm not sure the extent of George's initial injuries. However, I know while floating in the water, he was severely sunburnt. This is where I'm not sure which version of his story is correct; I've heard George say he removed his shoes, and I've also heard him say that his shoes and part of his clothing were blown off during the attack. Either way, the result was his feet got so badly sunburnt that after the rescue, he couldn't walk for a couple of weeks.

The Gambier Bay, the only US aircraft carrier sunk by surface shelling during the second World War, was named after a bay here in Alaska. The bay is located on Admiralty Island within the Admiralty Island National Monument, within the Tongass National Forest. In other words, not that far from where we live. We never visited the bay, but we've seen it from both the water and the air. Perhaps, if ALS hadn't gotten in the way, we would have made it there. I now hope that my grandsons will one day visit the bay and think of their great-grandfather.

In April of 2021, the press announced that the destroyer, USS Johnston (D557), also sunk during the Battle of Leyte Gulf, had been found at a depth of over 20,000 feet. As of May 2021, the hunt continues for the remains of the Gambier Bay.

Jap Shells Sink Carrier Under Denver Sailor

By LEWIS THOMAS
Rocky Mountain News Writer

A 19-year-old Denver bluejacket, George Durkop, gunner's mate third class, had a carrier shot out from under him but emerged from battle unscathed after a dunking in the ocean, a 50-yard swim and 46 hours on a wave-tossed life raft.

Durkop, a veteran of four major mix-ups with the Japanese in less than a year, now is home on leave. Yesterday he confessed with a grin that he's been scared "plenty of times," but never again wants to live through a nightmare like one off Leyte in October when Jap naval forces sent his carrier to the bottom.

"We knew there were some Japs nearby, but we sure were surprised one morning when a big portion of their fleet jumped us," Durkop said.

Big Shells Hit Vessel

"They scored several hits with big shells and set us afire. We put out one deck fire, but pretty soon things began to look hopeless. When the order came to abandon ship, I had neither time nor desire to rescue my gear, because shells were going through all parts of the ship. I just went over the side.

"I swam about 50 yards and managed to crawl up on a floating life net. I looked back and saw the third fellow in line behind me get plowed under by a heavy shell. I really got scared then."

Durkop and a few of his mates made it to a life raft, and then began a gruelling 46-hour "survival cruise" on the open sea.

Sent Home for a Rest

"Don't let anyone tell you a tropic night on the open sea isn't cold," Durkop said. "I guess we were lucky, though, because it rained a little and we managed to wring a little drinking water out of our clothes."

The sailors were picked up by an American naval patrol craft, hospitalized a short time for exposure and then sent home on leave.

Durkop figures he's been mighty lucky, but, at the same time, he insists he's had a few tough breaks. For instance, he regretted ruefully, when he lost his gear in the sinking, he lost every photograph he had, and most of them were pictures of Denver girl friends.

After he reached Denver, he discovered that his travels had taken him within sight of one and within eight miles of another of his army brothers, with none of the three the wiser. First Sgt. John is on Leyte, and Corp. Thoralf Jr. is in New Guinea.

George Durkop wears the American and Asiatic-Pacific Theater ribbons, with four bronze stars for major engagements in Guam, Saipan, Tinian and Leyte.

He is a son of Patrolman and Mrs. T. A. Durkop Sr., 3294 Newton st.

George Durkop

1944. Article about George Durkop in the Rocky Mountain News.

Dear Wife

22 November 2019

Preface: Death is a fact of life, but that doesn't make it any easier to talk about. In my life, I've witnessed too many deaths where the family has no idea what the deceased wanted. Therefore, I wrote this letter to my wife. Since I haven't been able to talk for the last four years, I had to type what I wanted to say. My fingers are also failing; communication is getting harder and harder. So, talking things over with my wife like we used to do is now a real challenge. Hence the letter.

Dear Wife,

I need to start by telling you that I love you. I spent my life making a ton of mistakes; however, the smartest thing I ever did was choose you as my lifelong partner. Thank you for putting up with me. And thank you for being you.

I should apologize for the burden my ALS is placing on you. It's not my fault, but that doesn't mean I don't feel bad about it. All those years ago, when you agreed to, "For better or worse," you surely didn't have any idea what that would mean in our golden years. This is not what I wanted for our retirement. Sorry.

I forget who said, "Death is no closer to the aged than the young," however, I take that to mean we have no idea when our time will be up. Or it could also mean anyone

one of us could die at any minute of the day. With that said, I'm relatively sure my time will run out long before yours does. I hope that is the case. I want you to be around for many more years. I know you always said you wanted us to go simultaneously, but I don't think that will happen. Since my breathing is getting more and more compromised with each passing week, I know that something as common as a cold could be the death of me. Or, like the other day when acid reflux brought a small bit of my stomach contents into my throat, and I aspirated a little into my lungs. I then spent the next couple of hours trying to clear that crud from my lungs. The risk is high with a cold or aspirating food to develop into pneumonia. And pneumonia is a common killer of people living with ALS. So odds are, I'll go before you. That's why I want to let you know a few things and my wishes before I pass.

My number one option is to donate my body to a medical school or somewhere that is doing ALS research. As you know, I've been looking into that for a while. The main obstacle seems to be we don't live in a state with a medical school. I'm going to keep searching. My second option is cremation. I know we talked about this a few days ago, and I mentioned that my research shows cremation uses the equivalent of two tanks of car gas, which equates to around 40-gallons of gasoline. Then there is transportation to the crematorium, so more energy is required. UGH. I know we also talked about burial at sea, and even though I was once in favor of that option, I no longer am.

It seems like my body would just become one more piece of litter in the ocean. The critters would eat my body, but there would still be things that don't get digested by the sea animals. Just the fact that there is a six-inch square of nylon mesh in my groin from a hernia surgery is enough for me to rule out a burial at sea. The last thing the ocean needs is more plastic, even if it's a small piece. Also, the wrapping of the body and weights required by law will be, in my opinion, something that doesn't belong in the ocean.

If I do get cremated, I'd like my ashes scattered on the top of one of the mountains near our home in Sitka. I wish for my ashes to migrate on the wind, landing in a steam and flow with the water, fertilizing new life on their journey to the ocean. The mountains with countless steams winding through the forests that hug the ocean shores of

Southeast Alaska are where I've always been the happiest. Knowing my ashes would be scattered on the top of one of our beautiful peaks gives me joy.

As for my belongings, you'll know best what to do with them. But this is my input. If possible, please donate all my handicap aids to the Evergreen Chapter of the ALS Association. If that is not possible, please donate them to Southeast Alaska Impendent Living (SAIL) or the Pioneer Home. Please continue doing what I've already been doing; give my tools to our son, Zach, or the grandsons. Everything else that is not of use to you, please donate to the nonprofit thrift shop, the White Elephant, or the Salvation Army.

Most important, after I'm gone, I want nothing more than for you to be happy. Part of happiness is human companionship. So if you find the right person, then, by all means, get involved in that relationship. I don't care, nor should you, what people think or say. Your happiness is more important to me.

One of the things I've missed the most since ALS hit me is being able to say, "I love you." I've also missed the hugs we used to give each other and holding hands as we did for so many years. I've especially missed the walks we used to go on, where we'd hold hands and talk about this and that. Remember when we used to end the day after the grandsons came for a visit, with conversations about them and how they are changing? I've greatly missed that.

ALS is a bastard disease, and I'm sorry it has taken so much from us. However, as bad as ALS has been, I've remained happy. I attribute that, in large, to you. You've taken excellent care of me while doing the many household chores I used to do. My ALS has forced you to become a carpenter, an electrician, a plumber, and even an auto mechanic. Not surprising to me, you've picked up those skills without hesitation.

Thank you for being the best wife ever.

Envy and Schadenfreude

29 November 2019

Envy:
- noun: A feeling of discontented or resentful longing aroused by someone else's possessions, qualities, or luck.
- verb: Desire to have a quality, possession, or other desirable attribute belonging to (someone else).

Schadenfreude:
- noun: Someone derives pleasure from another person's misfortune.

The other day on the podcast *Hidden Brain* by Shankar Vedantam, I heard the word schadenfreude. As you can see, the German word, with no exact English translation, means getting pleasure from someone else's misfortune. When I first heard the meaning of the word, I told myself that I would never gain pleasure from someone else's misfortune. But I have, and I do. One example they gave in the podcast was deriving pleasure when watching a rival sports team lose. Haven't we all gained satisfaction from watching our team win and our rivals lose? Or, how about our pleasurable giggle when we see the opposing team's quarterback being sacked? And, if that sack leads to an injury that sidelines that quarterback, we are even more joyous. So, I, too, can say that I also have experienced the pleasure of schadenfreude.

Shankar Vedantam started the podcast by talking about the Biblical Seven Sins: pride, greed, lust, envy, gluttony, wrath, and sloth. He then concentrated on envy and gave several examples of how envy can lead to schadenfreude. He cited the fictitious example of how happy Homer Simpson gets when his neighbor, Ned Flanders, whom he envies, is having hard times. Homer envies Flanders because he thinks Flanders has the ideal life, so when Flanders is facing bankruptcy, Homer finds pleasure in that. Hence, schadenfreude.

In my adult life I can't remember being envious of anyone. I might have been jealous that someone was able to go on a fun-filled weekend while I had to work. But, knowing my turn would come, I was never genuinely envious of that person. All in all, I was luckier than most. I have a loving wife who made me happy, a superb family and a dog that gives me joy. I don't live in a war zone or a refugee camp, have plenty to eat and a comfortable home. My friend who might have been having a fun weekend might have been stuck in a miserable marriage. And I would have never felt schadenfreude if that friend had suffered a hardship on his weekend.

I could feel schadenfreude if I found out someone like Syria's leader Bashar al Assad, who has killed tens of thousands of his own people, was afflicted with ALS. And I can think of more than one self-serving politician that I'd gain pleasure from if I heard he or she had ALS. However, I'd feel no pleasure in hearing if people like a neighbor who frequently sets off fireworks at all hours of the night keeping me from precious sleep, had a devastating disease. My greatest joy, perhaps considered schadenfreude, would be to see the ALS Monster suffer misfortune and ALS defeated. I'd be so happy at the death of the ALS Monster I'd dance on its grave.

Gasping for Air

6 December 2019

I wasn't sure if last night was a nightmare or reality. I woke up with my heart racing at double speed, and a full-on adrenalin rush. Even though I always sleep with my Trilogy machine, a noninvasive ventilator (NIV), I stopped breathing. I'd exhaled but didn't inhale until the adrenalin kicked my diaphragm into action. I then gasped as if I'd been doing a breath-holding free dive and nearly passed out from the lack of oxygen.

Sleep was history with that much adrenalin flowing through my body. A couple of minutes later, I had to pee, so I made the arduous trek to the bathroom. I say arduous because sitting up, then swinging my legs over the side of the bed, takes the better part of five minutes. Then another five minutes to go a dozen feet from the bed to the toilet. As I sat on the toilet, I wondered if I had just witnessed how I will die? With ALS sufferers, statistically, breathing failure is one of the leading causes of death. If so, dying in my sleep is how I'd always hoped to go.

A half-hour later, the adrenaline had subsided enough that I fell back asleep, albeit fitfully, waking often and wondering what lies ahead. Except for getting back slightly more movement out of my tongue, everything else with this ALS journey has been a downward slide. Bulbar ALS is often a rapidly progressing form of ALS. It's now six years since I first noticed symptoms. How much longer can I hold on? If I stop breathing again, will adrenalin once again kick in and save me?

As I said, I wasn't sure if what I experienced was reality or a dream, so I asked Connie if she heard me gasping. She said that she had and then heard me struggling to clear phlegm from my throat. Mucus is not only getting harder and harder to cough up, but when I do, it's hard not to choke on it. Pneumonia is another killer; will that be my ending? The panicking feeling when I can't breathe leads to a sense of doom. And, sometimes, I wonder if that feeling is worth it? That feeling is so strong, I wonder if death is preferable?

Behavior scientists' studies show most people aren't afraid of death; they are scared of the death process. I think that's true for me. Will there be pain? Or in my case, more than pain? Will I struggle to breathe? Suffocating is darn scary. I've come close to drowning several times, and my experience last night was scarier.

Meanwhile, I'm going to keep living life to the fullest. I'm going to continue loving my family and our little dog. I'm going to take comfort in tons and tons of good memories. ALS sucks, but life is still great, even if, from time to time, I get the bejesus scared out of me.

ALS Association Podcast Idea

18 February 2020

To: ALS Association, Media Relations

Fr: Marcel LaPerriere

I'm not sure I'm sending this to the correct department; however, media relations seem like it would fit. If not, please forward my email to whomever you think would be the appropriate person.

As a person living with ALS, I'm confined to a wheelchair. Also, like many people with ALS, my fingers don't work all that well, which makes turning pages to read a book nearly impossible. So, I listen to audiobooks and many podcasts, which brings me to why I'm sending you this email.

It seems to me there would be a place for podcasts dealing with ALS. And, who better to make them than the ALS Association? Podcasts could help raise awareness, educate, help people deal with ALS, help inform people of fundraising events, and even help raise funds. It's a given; podcast audiences would be limited. However, with an estimated 16,000 people in the USA alone living with ALS, plus their families, caregivers, and medical staff, the number of potential listeners in the USA alone could well be 200,000. If you include the English-speaking world, it is conceivable there could be over a million or more listeners. And in time, podcasts could generate revenue for the ALSA.

So, what would the podcasts cover? I'm glad you asked. I'll list just a few topics.

1. New research.
2. The research that the ALSA is funding.
3. New therapies and how they are working.
4. Interviews with people living with ALS.
5. Caregiving tips.
6. Caregiver burnout prevention.
7. Nutrition and supplements.
8. Accessibility issues.
9. Legislation.
10. Interviews with researchers.
11. Interviews with neurologists and other medical personal.
12. Transportation issues, from vans to public transportation, to airplanes.

The ALSA gets a lot of negative social media chat about how it only cares about itself and not the people it is supposed to serve. There are Facebook sites dedicated to bashing the ALSA, and I've heard about ALSA bashing on Twitter. Communication about what the ALSA is up to would go a long way towards squelching the negativity on social media.

Please consider producing podcasts. It could be beneficial for those of us living with ALS, and helpful for caregivers and medical professionals.
Thank you.

Postscript: I was delighted within an hour of sending this email, an ALSA Media Relations person responded, telling me that a podcast is in the works and will be out soon. Then in mid-March, they released the first podcast. As I write this postscript, it is mid-January 2021, and now that I have listened to all the ALSA podcasts that have so far been released, I'd give them a B+, with lots of room for improvement. The podcast is often informative; however, the two hosts don't seem to have their hearts into their work. From the interviews and voice inflections, they seem to be just passing time to earn a paycheck. As a longtime former boss of many employees, I can easily recognize when someone is doing just enough to get by, the two current hosts fit that bill.

Two Steps Down; a Half Step Back Up

26 February 2020

Most people living with ALS decline in what seems, metaphorically, like going down a set of stairs. If we are lucky, we might temporarily get a small step back up. That is how 2020 has gone for me.

Until the end of 2019, I was still dressing and undressing myself, getting on and off the toilet, in and out of bed, and transferring wheelchairs. I'm still doing some of those daily tasks, but with much more difficulty. Connie now has to help me dress. I still might be able to dress myself, but it would take far too much time and far too much energy. Shortly before the new year, I timed myself putting on one sock; seven minutes had passed. Today, I'd be lucky to do that same task in twice that amount of time. I wear special socks that Connie made me with zippers up the back, which makes putting them on easier. I haven't tried, but putting on a regular sock would now be impossible.

Just in the last week, I couldn't get into bed on my own. I had a very sore left hip and painful left hamstring tendon, and once they felt better, I could again swing my legs up onto the bed. Hence, the half step back up.

A couple of nights ago, the pain was bad enough that I couldn't get up out of bed to use the toilet. After struggling and failing several times, Connie got up, and with her help and several more failures, I was at long last able to get out of bed. Connie has now rigged a 3 to 1 pulley block and tackle to lift me out of bed, or into my wheelchair. Our sailing and caving experience is paying off with Connie knowing how to use the mechanical advantage with a 3 to 1 pulley system.

The pain in my left leg was due to straining my leg trying to roll onto my side in bed. Something as simple as turning over in bed is now nearly impossible. For close to two years, I've used a lower satin sheet to help in the task of rolling, and that magic has worked. Is it was now hindering me by not giving me anything to push against? We switched back to a cotton sheet, but it was like sleeping on Velcro; I couldn't move at all. Then I wondered about the convoluted foam mattress topper.Without the foam topper, turning was slightly more manageable, but the mattress was now only a bit more comfortable than a pile of rocks. The convoluted foam topper is back on the bed, and I've resigned myself to sleeping primarily on my back.

Sleeping only on my back increases the risk of pressure sores, especially on my heels. I've already had some mysterious issues with my heels, perhaps caused by poor circulation. The bottoms of my heels have been extra sore, red, and tender to the touch. Each morning, Connie helps me with my socks, and she rubs on a salve, cream, or ointment on them. We've tried zinc oxide, a prescription ointment called Triamcinolone Acetonide, another prescription treatment called Clotrimazole, and Betamethasone Dipropionate Cream, and Devil's Club salve. So far, nothing has worked, and I wake up each morning with inflamed and sore heels that improve slightly as the day wears on.

And what the doctors think started as a urinary tract infection (UTI) morphed into passing kidney stones. For about five weeks, I was urinating what looked like grit off a piece of 40 grit sandpaper. Sometimes, with each pee, I'd pass about a ¼ teaspoon of that grit. If you've never passed a kidney stone, then you've never experienced pain that is as bad as it gets. One doctor said to us that he's seen big-tough grown men lying on the floor curled up in the fetal position groaning in pain over kidney stones. If I could get down on the floor, I would have done the same. Tamsulosin's prescription drug helped, but surprisingly an over-the-counter medication for treating UTIs and turns urine fluorescent yellow-orange worked better than the Tamsulosin. I hope I never again experience that level of pain. I'd rather die.

This far into bulbar ALS, I'm darn lucky to be still eating by mouth, and I'm grateful for that. However, complacency has recently gotten me in trouble. Just a few days ago, eating some mac and cheese and not wanting to keep my face buried in my food, I looked up at Zach, which opened my windpipe. I swallowed and choked badly. For the first time, I felt food going down my windpipe and entering my lungs. Fortunately, after lots of coughing and a little puking, the noodle work itself back up and into my mouth. Choking that bad is scary and leads to feelings of panic and doom. I was done eating, even though I'd just started.

I should stop eating by mouth. It would be much safer. But, what fun is it to get one's nourishment by a feeding tube that bypasses one's taste buds? And when many people with ALS transition from eating by mouth to a feeding tube, exclusively, they seem to give up on living. I can totally understand why a person would give up without the simple joy of tasting their food.

Other declines include more loss of finger coordination. It's now nearly impossible to open a plastic food container, and typing is very slow. My hands now tremble most of the time, especially when I reach for something. All my toes except the big toes are curling under, adding to already sore feet. And, when I pull myself up to transfer chairs, use the toilet, or enter my bed, it takes several tries. It's as if the signal from my brain telling the muscles to get to work takes multiple times to connect. I get winded, even thinking about anything that takes muscle power. Then to make breathing even harder, I can no longer blow my nose.

I feel like I've taken two steps down and a half a step back up since the first of the year. As time progresses, there will likely more steps to descend. As much as I don't want to become an even bigger burden on Connie, we both know that considering I'm six years into this journey, it could and should be a lot worse. And even though I hate ALS with a passion, life is still good, and I'm happy.

As Bad as it Is

6 March 2020

As bad as it is living with ALS, it could be worse, much worse. Even when each day I see a further decline in body functions, I still feel lucky. I'm not living in a war zone; I don't have starving children I can't feed. I'm not watching my loved ones freeze to death in a refugee camp. I have a roof over my head, and if I get cold, I can turn up the heat or put on extra clothing. And, most important, I have a loving wife who takes care of me. I'm extremely lucky.

I got upset today when I saw some derogatory comments by a pALS on two different ALS Facebook sites. Since I only know this person by their Facebook page, I may have no right to be critical. When I look at photos of that person's house, I see a home that is as nice as mine. That person can still walk and talk, two things I can no longer do. Is that person bitter because they can't see their own good fortune, or are they wrapped in self-pity? I feel genuine sorrow for them if they can't see how good they have it. ALS sucks, but shouldn't we count our blessings and not dwell on the things that bring on bitterness? I sure think so.

Hunkered Down

26 March 2020

As Covid-19 spreads in parts of the US, most of us are hunkered down, trying to keep from getting the virus by social distancing and staying home. Living in a remote Alaska town makes us a bit safer than in Seattle, LA, or New York City. As safe as our little town is, we are still taking all the measures we can, especially since both Connie and I are in the high-risk category.

I wish there were a way to hunker down to keep the ravages of ALS from continuing to take its toll on me. This morning for the first time, Connie had to use the Hoyer Lift to get me out of bed and onto the toilet. And perhaps more devastating to me, I have no beard for the first time in over 30-years. Drool and other gunk continually flowing out of my mouth meant I always had a crusty beard. There is nothing wrong with being crusty at my age, but the crusty beard was getting to be too much. A shaved face will also make a better seal on my face-mask that I wear with my noninvasive ventilator (NIV). The shaved face doesn't make me happy, but it will make all the medical people who have been hounding for over two years to shave say, "It's about time."

Then there are hand tremors. Typing is now hard and sometimes nearly impossible. From time to time, I have to put one hand on the other to steady one hand enough to type. That slows down my typing to a snail's pace. Some drugs would help with the tremors, but I hate taking drugs. I'll probably take the drugs sometime in the future.

I hate ALS more and more each day, but I'm lucky to live where I do when I do. And, I'm fortunate to have such a wonderful wife. As I key this, she is up in her sewing room, modifying an old alpine climbing-harness to lift me in and out of bed. The harness that comes with the Hoyer Lift must have been left over from the Spanish Inquisition. It felt like something from a torture chamber. Maybe Hoyer was trying to make me spill the beans. Not only do I have nothing to spill, but with bulbar ALS, no torturing will make me talk. (A guy must have a little humor with ALS. It helps me stay sane.)

ALS sucks, but life is still good, even with no beard.

Procrastination

15 April 2020

Like everyone, I've been known to procrastinate, knowing full well some criti-cal things need to be done. However, when it comes to the must-do things, like changing the oil in our vehicles or cleaning a plugged downspout, I've always jumped right in. Now, I'd procrastinate long enough when I was in high school that I'd turn in an assignment late or never at all, which obviously affected my grades. Looking at the less than desirable grades on my report card taught me a lesson in life. When it comes to important things, there isn't much I hate more than procrastination.

Now that I'm living with ALS, I can no longer fix the plugged downspout or take the car to the mechanic to get the oil changed. Procrastination is not much of an issue for me anymore because I don't have many duties to procras-tinate about. Except the ultimate thing; dying. I have been procrastinating about that obligation, and am wondering if I should keep putting it off.

I'm not depressed, and all in all, I'm happy. But my ALS has progressed, to the point that even the simplest things have become overwhelming tasks. About a year ago, I started showering every other day because it was too taxing to do it daily. Even though it took a lot of effort to shower, I looked forward to it, and I'd wake up on shower days knowing I'd get the treat of a shower. Now, I dread shower days, not because I don't want to get clean or don't enjoy the warm water flowing over my body, but because it takes every ounce of my energy to get in, shower, and get out and dressed. On shower days, I feel as if I've started my day by running a full marathon.

And the medical literature that says there is little pain associated with ALS is 100% wrong. It might be easier to list the places that don't hurt than the places that do. Here's a list of places that hurt the worst, starting with my right shoulder. I've had a bum right shoulder for many years. Over 25-years ago, after an MRI, I was told I should have surgery for a torn rotator cuff. I put off shoulder surgery to the point that I'll never have it done. The orthopedic surgeon told me to expect a year to recover and six months of no work. I postponed the surgery so we could eat. Now, I depend on that arm and the other arm to lift myself on and off the toilet, so you bet that shoulder hurts.

Both of my heels which suffer painful pressure sores. We've tried everything, lamb's wool heel protectors, pillows under my ankles, and every salve and ointment known to humankind. My heels keep getting slowly worse and not better. I think the sores are caused by poor circulation. That I have to elevate my feet to relieve the constant swelling doesn't help the circulation in the small capillaries in my heels. At night, I'm often awakened by pain that feels like someone has placed the flame of a blow torch on my heels. And, I seem to have gout in my right big toe. I lie in bed agonizing over my heels, and my big toe feels like it is squeezed in a vice. Because of the pain and that I can't get comfortable, I rarely sleep more than an hour. I lie awake repeating the same thing over and over until the night at long last passes. The gout might be caused by poor circulation; I don't eat any of the foods associated with gout or drink any alcohol.

In bed at night my heels feeling like they are on fire, my toe is hurting like heck, my shoulder is aching, and my mouth is scorched dry by the Trilogy ventilator. I then try to roll on my side but can't, and I can't get comfortable enough to fall back asleep. It's these times that I wonder why I put off death. I'm not depressed or unhappy, but I am in pain. And with each passing week, I become a bigger burden for the woman I love. So, why the heck do I keep procrastinating? What indeed must come? I'm not contemplating doing anything crazy, but I wonder how much more I can take or will want to take?

I still say life is good, and more than ever, ALS sucks. For now, I'll keep on procrastinating what I know I can't put off forever.

Trilogy 100 Noninvasive Ventilator

22 April 2020

Recently, the Evergreen Chapter of the ALS Association held the first-ever men's only support meeting via Zoom. During that meeting, a couple of guys expressed how hard it was to get used to their Trilogy noninvasive ventilator. One man asked if anyone who uses a Trilogy could share some ideas on adapting to life using the Trilogy. I am no expert, but I have been using a Trilogy for more than a year. And, before that, I was using a Bipap for over two years.

One of the biggest complaints I have heard from people trying to get used to a Cpap, Bipap, or a machine like the Trilogy is the mask makes them feel claustrophobic. As a long-time scuba diver who even dabbled in cave diving, the one thing I didn't have to overcome was claustrophobia. So, unfortunately, I have no advice on overcoming claustrophobia. Maybe, like getting used to a scuba mask, it just takes time.

Speaking of masks, one of the challenges to using a Trilogy is finding the mask that works for you. I tried about a dozen masks before I found the ones that work for me. And the respiratory therapists, the pulmonologists, and others were right; to get a good fit, you'll need to shave your beard. I held out for over three years, and for the first time in more than three decades, I shaved. The last time I went without a beard was when I was learning to scuba dive. Not having a beard or mustache during the learning phase of scuba diving gave me one less thing to fight. After I got comfortable with my underwater skills, I grew my beard back. Bulbar ALS causes me to drool continually. Since I don't want to take medications to control drooling, it was time for the beard to go. And no beard means I can get a good fit on my ventilator mask.

Another complaint I've heard is the Trilogy feels like it's blowing too much air. A respiratory therapist told me that as a precaution, any respiratory therapist would set the inspiratory pressure a bit higher than may be required. It's better to have too much pressure than not enough. If you think you're getting too much air, work with your respiratory therapist, pulmonologist, or medical device representative, and ask them to adjust the inspiratory pressure down. With the Trilogy, you can do it yourself, but always make any adjustments working with your respiratory team.

We did make a couple of modifications without asking. First, my wife, Connie, made what I call the loincloth that covers the screen. Even though the screen can be set to auto darken, it takes three minutes, which are three minutes of light I don't want in the middle of the night when I get up to use the toilet. So, the loincloth keeps the room dark when we turn off the Trilogy or turn it back on. The other modification we did, was changing how the Fisher & Paykel MR810 humidifier gets its water. The medical equipment supplier had it set up so the humidifier is was supplied with sterile water from a hanging plastic IV bag. I didn't like the plastic taste gave to the water, and, what a waste to toss an IV bag in the trash every day or two. We took an old plastic water bottle, drilled a hole in the bottom, and installed a grommet that seals around the probe that is meant to be inserted into the IV bag. Connie then fills the water bottle with distilled water, which gravity feeds into the humidifier. This has worked better than I thought it would. I expected there to be a slight bit of water leakage, which there hasn't been, and, I figured we'd have to change the grommet every so often. We've used the same grommet for a year, and, even better, we've not had to throw away well over one hundred IV bags.

The best advice about getting used to their Trilogy ventilators I can give my fellow ALS friends is to give it time. Like everything new, over time, we get used to things until they become routine.

2020. The loincloth and water bottle with my Trilogy 100.

Postscript: When I posted the above on the Facebook site, Tips for Handicap Modifications, one woman said she got used to wearing her Trilogy mask by putting it on while watching TV or reading a book.

Covid-19

26 April 2020

Yesterday's news reported that our small island-bound town in the Alexander Archipelago of Southeast Alaska had its first confirmed case of Covid-19. Of course, I was worried about the unfortunate person contracting the disease, and genuinely feel sorrow for everyone involved in this first case.

This case was a patient in the Long-Term Care Unit of the Southeast Alaska Regional Health Consortium's (SEARHC) hospital. Extra precautions have been taken there, so the experts are scratching their heads about how the virus entered the facility. Our somewhat isolated town can only be accessed by plane or boat. Air travel is about 5% of normal, and the last ferry stop was October of last year. Our governor placed a fourteen-day self-quarantine order for everyone coming into Alaska about a month ago. Did someone come to Sitka in the last month not self-quarantine? Or did they quarantine in a house where family and friends were coming and going? Or perhaps a crew-person on a fishing boat from Ketchikan, Juneau, or even Puget Sound came ashore, went to the grocery store, and gifted the deadly virus to our town. Or did a crew-person on one of the sea-going barges that bring us food and fuel pass it to a person onshore? And was the unwitting carrier of the virus asymptomatic?

Perhaps the even bigger mystery to solve is how did the virus enter the long-term care facility? And how did the person who brought it into the facility catch it? Visitations there have been restricted for the past month, so how the heck did it enter the building? Was it a healthcare worker, or perhaps someone in housekeeping or food services? Or possibly a maintenance worker doing a routine task, like changing a lightbulb? Or did a delivery person bringing medication, food, or something else, unwittingly bring the virus into the building? Contact tracing can be very challenging.

As a senior living with ALS, if I fell victim to Covid-19, it would be curtains for me. And though my wife, Connie, who is over the Medicare age and in better shape than many people half her age, has suffered allergies and asthma her whole life, which puts her into a higher risk category. With all the pollen in the air this time of year, she has enough trouble breathing. I depend on Connie for almost everything, so I'd be in a world of hurt without her, and would probably end up in the long-term care unit. So I worry about Connie catching this novel virus, too.

Maybe now that the virus has come to our town people will take it more seriously? This past last week, I've seen what looks like total complacency; people barbequing with friends - kids playing with their friends. We even saw a large tour-boat with about forty people onboard heading out on a cruise.

I'm tired of self-isolation, and I'm extra worried about the small businesses in our town. Many of them will not survive the shutdown. And what about the loss of jobs and sales tax revenue that funds city services? Since our town depends on the summer tourist season which we will not have, I fear the worst is yet to come.

Since we are at least a year away from a vaccine, will governments be forced to decide that 5% of the population must be sacrificed to develop unproven herd-immunity? Will they open business too soon to save the economy? Will Connie and I be part of the collateral damage? Or will some of my family or friends be the ones who are sacrificed? As with any war, what will be an acceptable loss of life? Can we declare victory if our governments decide to sacrifice the vulnerable?

ALS puts me in the extra high-risk category for Covid-19. I'm living on borrowed time. Given those facts, if it would do any good and hasten the course of this virus, I'd be the first to sacrifice my life to save an economy for my grandsons and their generation. What I fear the most is dying alone, like most who are dying from this terrible virus are. That is the saddest thing about Covid-19.

Postscript: The man who first tested positive later tested negative, so the test might have been a false positive. Since the test results took six days to return from the lab, we still know nothing until the man is tested for Covid-19 antibodies.

A second case was reported on Memorial Day and was said to be an asymptomatic carrier. That case was a young woman between the age of 18 to 29. She had gone for a medical appointment for some unrelated health concern and was given the test.

A third case reported on the 4th of June was not counted as a case in Sitka because the man had traveled from somewhere outside the state. That man was demonstrating many of the typical symptoms when he was tested.

By the end of 2020, Sitka reported almost 300 cases and no fatalities. And the vaccine arrived in our small town the week before Christmas.

You Look Good

12 October 2018

"You look good," is a phrase I hear often from both friends and family. They are right –– I do look good and healthy. Aside from having ALS, I'm in fairly good health. But, I'm far from good. No one with advancing ALS can be considered to be in good health.

With ALS is there will always be more and more declines. What's not given is the timing of those declines. There could even be small improvements. In my case, the improvements never seem to last much more than a couple of weeks. ALS is different for everyone. There are no two cases exactly alike.

As we approach the six-week mark of our road trip vacation, I've noticed that despite the fact we are having fun, my decline is marching on. I'm having a harder time standing, transferring from my power chair to my manual wheelchair, getting in and out of bed, and even getting off and on the toilet. I also continue to lose dexterity in my fingers. Simple little things like grabbing a single napkin out of a stack is now a real challenge. And to tie my shoes, I must lift one leg at a time with my arms onto a stand to reach my shoes.

The saying goes, "Getting old is not for wimps." That applies double for ALS. Another saying goes, "It beats the alternative." That is true for both.

I hate the continued decline caused by a neurological disease that I have no control over. But I control my attitude about facing a disease that will continue to steal abilities from me. As the ALS Monster continues to take, I will not let it give me bitterness, depression, anger or any other negative emotions. It scares the daylights out of me, but I'll live life as fully as I can each and every day. I'll take, "You look good," as a compliment. Then, do my best to look good inside.

Just Another Adventure

18 June 2020

Just Another Adventure is the title of my first book about living with ALS, and *The Adventure Continues* is the title of my second book. After a lot of debate, my third book in the trilogy will be titled, *The Last Adventure*. I hope my writing will help others living with ALS. Through book sales, I also hope to generate a few dollars that we can donate to ALS nonprofits. Writing is also therapeutic for me and the only way I can be creative. I haven't been able to speak since the beginning of 2016, and I haven't been able to build or repair things since the summer of 2017. I've always needed some creative outlet, and today, it is writing.

I mentioned the book titles because they may be confusing, even insulting, to some. Recently, when I was promoting my first two books on a Facebook ALS site, a lady wrote these words. "I'm confused. I don't think my husband found it an adventure; it was Hell from the day he was diagnosed to the day he literally choked to death. A living nightmare, and so cruel." I can't argue with those words? She was obviously writing from the heart. This was my response. "I have to look at living with ALS as an adventure, or I'd be depressed all the time. I've come close to choking to death more times than I can count. Choking is darn frightening, and since I have bulbar onset ALS, choking is a part of daily life. I still live as adventurous a life as I can. I've taken my wheelchair places others won't walk. So, yes, ALS is just another adventure for me. It's not one I'd choose or wish on anyone, but for my sanity, I'll keep looking at ALS as an adventure."

I look at ALS that way for a couple of reasons. First, others are living with challenges much greater than mine. I tried to count the times I've come close to death, but had to give up. Once when rock climbing as a teenager I came within feet of cratering at the base of the cliff. Another time when I was in my 20s, I fell sixty feet into a crevasse on Mount Rainer. And twice I nearly drowned cave diving. I also came close to drowning when I was five. What about the severe reaction I had to penicillin in the fall of 2015? That time my blood pressure fell to 40/20, and the blood tests showed my kidneys and liver were shutting down. In the 90s a man held a loaded AR-15 with the safety off a foot from my belly. If my good friend Tom Fouts hadn't intervened, I might not be here today. Not listed above are the many, many beatings as a child that should have killed me. And never mind the close calls I've had flying in small airplanes and helicopters here in Alaska. So to me, ALS, is just another adventure.

When Zach was seven or eight, Connie started reading him C. S. Lewis' seven-book series *The Chronicles of Narnia*. While Connie read, I would sit and listen, and over time, I got more into the books than Zach did. I'd beg Connie to keep reading when she'd stop, and before Zach and I knew it, Connie had read six of the seven books to us. Then, I read and reread all the books for myself. When I got to book seven, *The Last Battle*, I understood why Connie hates the last book in the series and refused to read it to us. One of my favorite characters in the books is the fearless little mouse, Reepicheep. We first meet Reepicheep in the second book, *Prince Caspian*. And book three, *The Voyage of the Dawn Treader*, couldn't be told without Reepicheep; he and his companions partake on a sailing voyage of adventure, exploring the very ends of their world. He is fearless and will take on foes many times his size. He loves an adventure, and there is nothing more important than his honor. At the end of the third book, when the sailing ship, the *Dawn Treader*, can go no further, Reepicheep volunteers to break a spell that has been cast on the entire crew by going on alone in his small coracle to the very end of their world. As Reepicheep waves goodbye to the others, he knows he can never return. He holds his head high and fearlessly embraces what he considers the ultimate adventure.

Reepicheep is a fictional character but, he exemplifies traits I admire: courage, honesty, honor, and the love of a good adventure. I look at ALS as an enormous beast that I'd wish not to confront. However, I'll continue to put on a stiff upper lip and face the Monster as Reepicheep would. I'll do my best to honestly express my feelings of gratitude for the care my wife and family provide me; like Reepicheep, that would be the honorable thing to do. And, for my sanity, I'll continue to look at my ALS journey as an adventure, right up until I face the ultimate adventure, death. If Reepicheep were real, I'd want him to be proud of me.

Things That Make You Go, Humm

24 June 2020

As a nutrition supplement, I use a liquid food called Compleat - spelled wrong. The food is liquid, and it goes directly into my stomach via a feeding tube. Compleat is packed with all the vitamins, minerals, and protein that a person needs to survive. In just 8 oz, it has 265 calories. Since I can still get most of my nutrition by mouth, I only take 4 oz a day to augment my hydration and add a few calories. In time I'll probably need more liquid food to survive.

A doctor's prescription is needed to buy most liquid food formulas, and Medicaid and the insurance companies will only pay for Compleat or any other liquid food when it becomes 100% of a person's nutrition. Why do we need a prescription when I'm only using it for a few additional calories and nutrition? I don't want to rely on it and don't enjoy having food pumped into my stomach. It's not like it is addictive. So why the prescription and lack of insurance coverage?

Envisioning Connie running a black market selling a controlled substance in some dark alley makes me laugh. As her customer approaches, she opens her long coat to reveal some really good liquid food. In a shaky voice, she says, "Hey man, I've got some Compleat. You can have it for $3.99 a box." As the deal is about to go down, here comes Sitka's Finest, with guns drawn. "Okay, get your hands up where we can see them;" "You there, drop the goods." When Connie looks their way, she asks, "Me?" And the cops say, "Yeah, you grandma, drop the goods and get your hands up, NOW!"

Why? I just don't get it.

Postscript: When I posted a version of this on Facebook, our pharmacist said in over three decades, he has yet to figure out why Medicare requires prescriptions for some things. If it is a mystery to him, I have reason to scratch my head.

An Amazing Gift

July 17, 2020   Zach's 47th Birthday

Some judge happiness by the material things they acquire. A bigger house with lots of furnishings, art hanging on the walls, and embellishments on every surface. Maybe a new car every year. Or possibly purchasing a new outfit of clothing brings them joy. A woman I once knew who owned well over fifty pairs of shoes. Buying shoes must have brought her happiness. Who the heck needs that many shoes?

What brings me happiness is my wife and family. And the silly beagle we named Bella. That dog makes me laugh when I get up in the morning until I go to bed at night. Even during the night, I often laugh at her snoring or other nighttime antics.

In the past a new tool, or a new piece of outdoor gear would make me darn happy. A new SkilSaw with a new blade cutting into a beautiful piece of locally grown lumber to build something functional would make me happy. And I'd be ecstatic knowing a brand-new drysuit was going to keep me warm and dry during my next scuba dive. But none of those compares to the happiness I get recalling memories I've been lucky enough to make with Connie over the last forty-eight years.

When Connie's father, George, passed away in 2005, Connie traveled to Colorado to help her mother, Millie, and brother, Scott, pack Millie's pared-down belongings for her move to Alaska. During that process, she noticed a box labeled in her father's handwriting, "Connie's Letters." She didn't give it much thought at the time and packed it with dozens of other boxes. In Sitka, we stored Millie's goods in a storage locker while we finished the house we were building for Millie, Connie, and me. In 2007 when we moved Millie into the house, "Connie's Letters" were moved, but remained unopened until after Millie died in 2013. When Connie was settling her parent's estate, she mentioned the box to me. At the time, while I was busy working long days I forgot about them. Connie, as is her fashion, was fanatically organizing paperwork, and put her old letters in four, full, four-and-a-half-inch-thick binders.

Fast forward to about a month ago. I was writing about our second sailboat, *Sea Dragon*, and the trip we took in it up the Inside Passage to Alaska in 1983. I asked Connie to get me the *Sea Dragon* log, and she suggested there might be something in her letters about the trip. And sure enough, there was an 18-page letter about the journey! It was like striking gold. Not only did it help me remember many things I wouldn't have, but it brought back a lot of oh-so-valuable memories.

That 18-page read and reread letter sparked my interest, so, a few days ago, when I asked Connie to read me a bedtime story, I wanted her to read her old letters to me. Though I could read them myself, it's much more fun to relive the memories with the woman I love.

Connie started with the first letter, dated September 1972. Even reading four or five letters a night, we are only up to mid-1975. With each letter, a ton of good memories flood my brain. In one letter Connie told her parents about the new crib we'd bought a couple of months before Zach was born. Missing from the letter was our purchase of a little stuffed dog, as well. And the memory of that stuffed toy took me on a long walk down memory Lane.

At times I lie in bed at night, trying to fall back asleep by ignoring the unbearable pain in my tail bone and back. If anyone tells you ALS is a pain-free disease, please tell them they are full of beans. Anyway, as I adjusted the hospital-type bed up and down, and wiggled trying to get the weight distributed so that the pain wouldn't be so intense, I thought of the little stuffed dog and how it got its name. The tag sewn to the toy said, "My name is Roger." Roger he was, until one day Connie called him Norman. One of the guys I worked with was named Roger Norman. We got a good laugh at that, and Norman seemed to fit the little dog better. Zach couldn't say Norman early on, but he could say Nor-Nor. So Nor-Nor, he was, and still is today.

Connie once had to bake Nor-Nor in the oven. No, she was not trying to be Wicked Witch of the West, who'd bake little kid's stuffed toys. Nor-Nor had it coming; that baking and a needle and thread possibly saved his life. Nor-Nor had nearly drown while trying unsuccessfully to be a long-distance Olympic swimmer in the bilge of *Destiny*, a friend's boat we lived on for a month while our newly-built boat, *Nimbus*, was in for some warranty work. Zach was two and a half, and Nor-Nor somehow escaped from his bunk and dived, I assume headfirst, into the murky water of the bilge. After a couple of days searching the 45-foot boat for the missing bedtime snuggle toy, I lifted the floorboards and found it floating face down in oily bilge water. Worse, he was already in the process of decomposing, as some stuffing was bulging out of a seam. That's where the talented hands of a loving mother came to save the day.

While Zach and I looked on, the miracle-maker mom first gave the drowned and decomposing Nor-Nor a bath in soapy dishwater. Then, Nor-Nor was placed on a rack inside the already hot Dickenson diesel stove with the oven door left open, and soon there was the scent of a drowned stuffed dog whiffing through the cabin. After baking for nearly an hour, Nor-Nor had his guts crammed back into his innards, and was skillfully stitched back together by Dr. Mom. NorNor was as good as new, and most importantly, a little boy had his snuggle puppy back.

After I adjusting the bed and wiggling a bit more, I slept and dreamt of Nor-Nor, a happy little boy and a loving mother. What an amazing gift Connie's father left us when he saved all of Connie's letters. Connie was a prolific letter writer and a good daughter who loved her parents. Her letters and that her father must have treasured them re-flame old memories. Those memories helped me overcome the pain and fall back to sleep when I needed the rest. I wouldn't trade those memories for a billion dollars.

ALS sucks, but as long as I can keep withdrawing good memories from deep in my memory bank, I'll be happy as anyone on Earth. Thank you, George, for saving all those letters. They bring this old man more joy than I could ever express.

2020. My grandson, Nate, took this photo of Nor-Nor as he looks today. He is sporting a hat and vest made by Connie.

Sorry, You Have ALS

16 August 2020

In a recent dream, a man in a white lab coat that I assume was a doctor, said to me, "Sorry, you have ALS-always-laughing-syndrome. It's very contagious, and can spread easily to others. In this time of a worldwide pandemic, it's what we need." He then said, "Oh, you have the other kind of ALS, too. Don't worry, it isn't contagious."

I was laughing when I woke up. I do have both kinds of ALS, but what's wrong with always-laughing-syndrome? The more contagious it is, all the better. In today's world of endlessly depressing news, we need more laughing. And living with the authentic form of ALS, I need more laughing to keep my sanity. If you agree we all need a good laugh and don't already have one, get a dog. I know our fat little beagle, Bella, keeps me laughing 24-hours a day. It doesn't have to be a beagle. Oscar, the small mixed-breed imp-dog who lives next door can make me laugh at least as much as Bella can. The other night I laughed out loud watching Oscar nipping and eating both ripe and unripe strawberries, of all things, from our planter boxes. Connie said, "He's going to have the runs if he eats many more." We both laughed, knowing he might pay for robbing us of our strawberries. It was worth the laugh.

Another evening Oscar kept going out to the lake in front of our houses. The lake has several feet of a grassy and muddy marsh along the shore before you reach the water. Oscar parted the grass in the marsh and soon became an absolute mud puppy. I laughed, but it likely horrified his owners, the best neighbors ever. The little imp-dog probably went right into the bathtub after his romp in the swamp.

I do indeed suffer from ALS-always-laughing-syndrome. It's fantastic medicine for the real ALS. Without it, it would be hard to keep the blues at bay.

Amyotrophic lateral sclerosis sucks, but aways-laughing-syndrome is what makes life worth living.

2020. Oscar was eating strawberries after his romp in the marsh.

Total Dedication

13 September 2020

She should have arrived on Tax Day, the 15th of April 2014, but some problem in the airfreight department at the Yakima Airport delayed the shipment one day. April 16th, we met the Alaska Airlines afternoon flight at the Sitka Airport, which brought a little fur-ball, the beagle we named Bella, into our lives. If you'd told me that afternoon how much a person can get attached to a dog, I I wouldn't have believed you. I grew up with dogs, cats, horses, cattle, and other animals, and, in the late 70s to the early 80s, we owned three different beagles. Though I liked and even loved a lot of those animals, Bella has wormed her way deeper into my heart than any other animal I've been associated with.

That same warm April day Bella came into our lives, had anyone told me that my voice cracking each evening for the last couple of months was one of the first symptoms of ALS, I would have said, "No way. It's just all the cedar sawdust I've been breathing." Yellow cedar dust gave me asthma-like symptoms, and adding red cedar dust into the mix was a reasonable explanation of why my throat felt all scratchy. From years of house building and woodworking, I knew a scratchy throat was a common side effect of working with wood. And the best remedy and cure was to get out into the woods and on the trails. Fresh air was the best way to clear out my lungs. We had a climbing trip to the Italian Dolomites and the French Pyrenees coming up, and I wanted to be in shape. Since I'd probably be the old guy in the group, and didn't want to hold anyone up, every time we had a chance, we hit the hills.

When the Europe trip came that August, I was far more worried about Connie getting over her bout with sarcoidosis than my ever-worsening throat problems. I'd be away from sawdust in Europe, and Connie showed every sign of bouncing back to her usual self.

When we met the rest of our climbing group, as we suspected, we were the group's seniors. And within a day, we also observed we were in the best shape of the group. Connie and I, with little effort, were always at the head of the pack. Connie figured she was doing so well because she was still on a moderate dose of the steroid prednisone. And I just felt lucky to be still the strongest hiker and climber of the group, something I'd been used to ever since I was in my teens.

Though I was far away from the cedar sawdust, Europe seemed to accelerate what I now know is ALS. Also, we both missed what Connie affectionately calls our PITA dog. In just a few months, we'd learned our Bella could be a real pain in the ass. But even as a full-fledged PITA, she had already wormed her way deep into our hearts. As much as we were enjoying everything about Europe, for the first time on vacation, we looked forward to getting home. We missed our grandsons and the little PITA dog.

Right after we got Bella, Connie declared, "No way that dog is ever sleeping in our bed." The night I broke that rule, I saw a little crying puppy's big brown eyes looking up at me, telling me she wanted up on our bed. I could also hear Connie saying, "You know if you pick her up and put her on the bed, there is no going back?" I picked her up, placed her between us, and was immediately rewarded with a happy tail-wagging puppy who quickly fell fast asleep.

By the time we went back to Europe in August of 2016, we'd made around a dozen trips to Seattle for my medical care. On many of those trips, we boarded Bella with our son, Zach, or Connie's good friend, Myrna. Most were short trips, but in October of 2015, we were gone nearly a month. We always missed our three grandsons and Bella and scrolled through the photos of them on my iPhone. That helped ward off homesickness. As we scrolled through photos, we'd count down the day and hours, and then, when we got on the plane, we'd count down the minutes until we'd get to see the boys and Bella. Looking at the photos made the separation a bit more bearable and the reward of getting home even sweeter.

I always looked the forward to Bella's welcome when we returned. With an excited wagging tail that always extended along her whole body, Bella never disappointed us. An after nearly a month in the hospital, Bella's wagging tail, excited jumps, and even her slobbery licks were the best welcome home ever. Absence does makes the heart grow fonder, and when it came to Bella, this was doubly so. Besides just seeing her, I always looked forward to a snuggle puppy, even if it meant a paw or two in my face as I slept.

By March of 2018, the ALS had progressed to the point I could no longer walk without a walker, and stairs became impossible. That meant we had to move from our upstairs master bedroom to the bedroom right off our first-floor kitchen. My ever-progressing ALS also meant that in order to breathe while I slept, I'd have to move from the bed I shared with my wife and the cute little snoring beagle to a hospital-type bed. At first, our two beds were side by side, and I could sometimes reach over to pet Bella. But ALS never stops progressing, and to have enough room for a Hoyer lift that is sometimes needed to lift me in and out of bed, Connie had to move the two beds into a T shape.

That meant I could no longer reach the little dog to give her a scratch behind the ears. However, I still enjoyed hearing the little PITA dog snoring. And when Connie got up to use the toilet at night, and return to find that PITA sleeping on her pillow, I'd laugh. A real PITA. But it's kind of funny. When nature calls, the wolf descendant not only takes over the bed but dares to commandeer your pillow.

On the 25th of August while I napped, Connie and Bella walked to the dog park, or as we've come to call it, the bark park. There is nothing Bella loves more than to chase balls, and knowing no patience, she barks her head off until a ball is thrown for her to chase. But being a hunting dog and not a retriever, she doesn't bring the ball back. So Connie's routine is to throw a ball, and while walking towards that ball that Bella chased but not retrieved, throw a second ball. This day, Connie threw the second ball, and Bella just sat there, not running or barking. Something was wrong; Bella would literally chase balls until she dropped, and this was only the second ball she had thrown. As Connie walked towards Bella, the little dog looked up as if to ask, "What just happened?"

When I woke from my nap I saw Connie carrying Bella in her arms. She said, "I have to call the vet because Bella can't walk." We were both relieved that the vet could see Bella in 15 minutes."

Another symptom of bulbar ALS is uncontrollable emotions. I cried as Connie carried Bella out to the vet. The vet thought she might have torn a muscle in her left hind leg and to give it a couple of days to see if she recovers.

It was apparent Bella was in a lot of pain. She didn't want to move, eat, or go outside to do her business. Connie carried Bella to bed, and as I drifted off to sleep, I was happy to hear her snoring. About 11:00 p.m. we woke to a big bang. As I woke up, I heard Connie on the floor, comforting Bella, who, for the first time, had fallen out of bed. Connie figured she tried to stand to change positions. Her legs gave out and she fell. To prevent this from happening again, out came a foam pad, and Connie and Bella slept the rest of the night on the floor. We knew then that the two would end up sleeping on the floor for the foreseeable future.

Two days later Bella was limping worse than ever, so she went back to the vet. This time the vet did a full series of X-rays, and there was good and bad news. The good news was that her spine was fine. And, the bad news, Bella had torn the cruciate ligaments in both hind legs. I cried, both from the bad news and from watching the poor dog trying to walk.

Bella was going to take months to get better. Three days after she got hurt, Connie had Zach, Jenn, and Nate help her move the couch upstairs to our old master bedroom and the mattress from Connie's bed onto the living room floor where the sofa had been.

For a dog that, in Connie's words, was never going to sleep in our bed, Bella now has a full-sized double bed on the living room floor and a human mama who cuddles up with her; one lucky dog and one very dedicated dog owner. Our living room windows don't have any shades. Winter's long hours of darkness will help with sleeping there, while midsummer, with around 20 hours of daylight, sleeping won't be so easy for Connie. I hope that Bella is better by the spring equinox, and Connie and Bella are back to sleeping in the same room as I do.

At three weeks post-her injuries, Bella is getting a little bit better. She is walking a little bit more each day, and she appears to be in less pain. On our daily walks, when she has reached her walking limit, she hitches a ride on my lap. Connie made a plywood dog-carrying platform that sits on my lap and straps to my power wheelchair. Bella seems to enjoy the higher vantage point. She can look around, sniff the air, and can still bark at squirrels. And I get a kick out of her riding on my lap on my chair. It gives me a chance to see her up close as she interacts with the world, and I can pet her we motor along the path, trail, or sidewalk.

Since we got Bella about the same time I developed ALS, and since the life expectancy of a person living with ALS is usually under five years, I always thought I'd die way before Bella would. I still hope that is the case. I'm not sure emotionally I could face losing her. Just as I couldn't face losing Connie, the dedicated person who takes care of a little dog and me. I'm selfish in this regard, but please let my one selfish wish come true. Meanwhile, I'll keep my fingers crossed that both Bella and I beat the odds, Bella heals without surgery, and I keep kicking for a few more years.

2020. Bella looks like she is sad and in pain a few days after her accident. She is lying on the mattress on the living room floor.

Postscript: Bella did get better without surgery. Within four months of her injury, she was running a bit, and by six months, she was about 95% back to normal. Because of her forced diet, which didn't make her very happy, she lost about eight pounds, which helped her heal.

Connie found she slept better away from the noise and lights emitting from my Trilogy. Plus, the poor sleep I get causes me to wiggle and the springs on my bed sound like a squeaky door. So, the two girls decided to keep their bed in the living room. Connie sleeps light enough she can still hear if I need help. And just because I sleep poorly, doesn't mean the girls don't deserve a good night's sleep.

2020. Connie made this plywood carrier so Bella could ride while she healed. She'd walk a little, then she'd communicate by looking up that she wanted a ride. She seemed to like hunting squirrels from her perch on my lap.

Erythema Multiforme

14 October 2020

Facebook reminded me that five years ago today a bad reaction to amoxicillin came close to killing me. The antibiotic, given to me after transsphenoidal surgery to remove a tumor on the pituitary gland, caused me to experience the misery of erythema multiforme, a painful and very itchy skin disorder. After a week in the ICU and being told I was lucky to be alive, I now have a better idea of what people experiencing Covid-19 live through.

That also means I'm now well over six years into living with ALS, actually, closer to 7-years. ALS continues to rob me of body mobility, but I'm beating the odds. Most people with ALS don't live this long. ALS SUCKS, but life continues to be good.

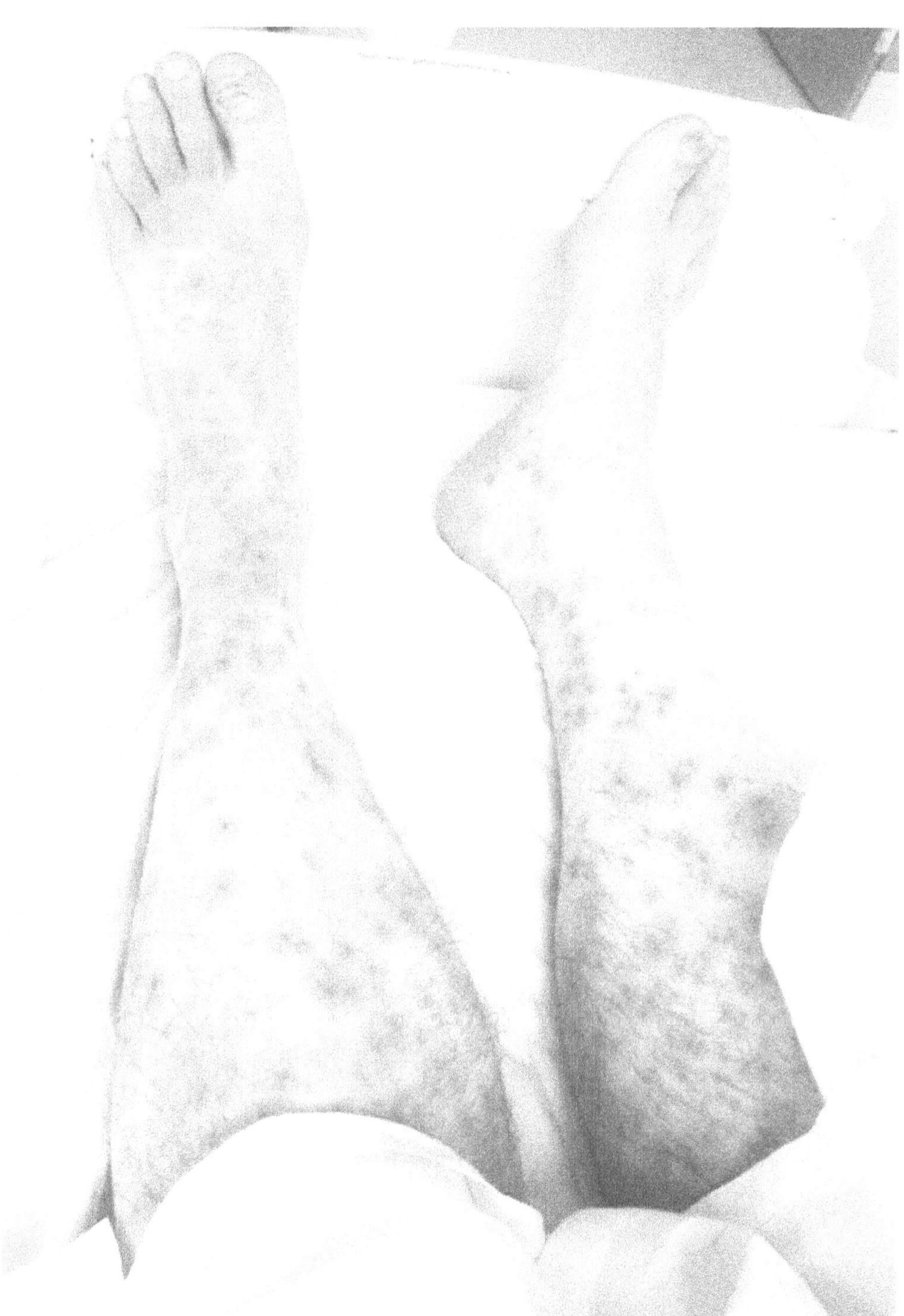

2020. The rash covered every inch of my body. I think you can see why it was so painful and itchy.

Soda Pop

29 December 2020

Even as a kid, I never was much of a soda pop drinker. So, why in the heck would I be thinking and writing about pop? Recently I posted a story on Facebook a about a junior high teacher. As a way to demonstrate just how big a million is, she had her students collect a million pop-bottle caps. Those caps filled about a 120-cubic-foot storage room.

I've been thinking about all the kinds of sodas we had available to us as kids. In the 1950s and '60s, we may have had more varieties of pop than there are now. Nowadays there are flavored waters, vitamin water, energy drinks, sports drinks, and many types of fruit juice we could have only dreamed of then. Take pomegranate juice. Heck, when we were kids, if we were extra lucky, we might get to share a pomegranate once a year. Yet today, you might find half a dozen different types of pomegranate juice on the grocery store shelves, not to mention all the other juices unavailable when I was a kid.

Now, there are healthier beverage options than we had, not that soda pop isn't still a big seller. Looking at the obesity problem we have now and that we didn't have when I was a kid, I wouldn't be surprised if, per capita, there are more sugary drinks sold today than there were in the '60s. Early one morning three or four years ago, waiting while Connie was grocery shopping, I noticed a father with a somewhat chubby daughter, maybe age ten, enter the store. As they walked to their car maybe ten minutes later, the father was drinking a Red Bull, and the daughter was eating a large candy bar and carrying a 12-ounce bottle of pop; what I assume was her before-school breakfast.

Note how the bottle is all scuffed up. There was a bottle return deposit in Colorado, and after washing, the bottles were repeatedly used. You could always tell how used the bottles were by how scuffed up they were.

In my youth, a soda pop would be reserved for a hot afternoon or a special occasion, and we had several options to choose from. We had Coca-Cola and Pepsi, which I preferred over Coke. There was also the less expensive option, RC Cola, which wasn't very popular with the kids I knew. Then there was 7UP and a new, at the time, drink called Sprite. Anytime we were sick, out came either Canada Dry or Schweppes ginger ale, both of which I liked. But my favorite was Hines or Dad's root beer, or, even better, A&W. We'd go to an A&W to get a large glass mug of root beer on special occasions or, if we were extra lucky, a root beer float. And being from Denver, there was the local brand, Duffy's, which, even as a kid, I found way too sweet. I almost forgot Bubble Up, which was a substitute for 7UP, and Crush, an orange flavored soda and grape soda. Both were too sweet. And how could I forget one of my favorite pops, Dr. Pepper, with the numerals 10, 2, and 4 that circled the words Dr. Pepper on the pop-bottle label. Dr. Pepper was hinting that they'd like you to drink their pop at 10:00, 2:00, and 4:00. We also see Nehi (pronounced: Knee High) soda pop advertisements. I don't think it was available in Denver and I don't I ever remember drinking any.

The famous 10, 2, and 4 on every Dr. Pepper bottle.

One of my earliest memories is of my mother loading up my two older brothers, my older sister, and me into her Nash Rambler station wagon and taking us to an A&W for root beer floats one hot summer day. I must have been only three or four at the time. Since A&W was a big treat, we were probably celebrating my older brother Fred's birthday since it falls in August.

In the winter of 1972, my senior year in high school, I lived with my older brother, Fred, and his wife, Kay. Fred was the Vice President of Denver Burglar Alarm (DBA), which had around one hundred employees. Unlike most VPs in a company that size, Fred would have been just as comfortable turning wrenches in the auto shop, where they serviced DBA's 80-some vehicles. He could have just as easily been out on fire or burglar alarm service calls as sitting behind a desk. He was a hands-on type of manager. That's why one freezing cold weekend, I found myself helping Fred and a couple of other DBA employees dig a two-hundred-foot-long ditch in some solidly frozen ground.

When Denver's Stapleton Airport was built in 1929, it was way out in the sticks. By 1972, several businesses were filling in the agricultural land near the airport with warehouses and offices. One warehouse was for Canada Dry, where DBA installed both the burglar and fire alarms. By 1995, Stapleton was much too small, and Denver's airport was moved further east to where Denver International Airport is located today.

Back to digging the ditch. Somehow or someone forgot to run an underground wire alongside the 6-inch water main pipe between the fire hydrant, which was located out on the street, to the new Canada Dry warehouse/distribution center. So the pipe had to be dug up. The pipe was buried five or six feet deep, and many yards of fill-dirt had been brought into level off the area that would become the building's parking lot. And each layer of fill that had been imported one foot at a time, froze solid as a rock. For two days, we tried in vain to dig deeper than a couple of feet. We poured diesel fuel in the ditch, and lit it on fire, hoping the fire would heat the ground an inch or two, but it didn't.

We rented industrial flame-throwing weed burner, and still not an inch was gained. Pick and shovel worked best, but it was a futile effort until the ground warmed up. In typical Denver fashion, the weather got sunny and warm the next week, and the ground thawed enough to get the ditch dug and the missing wire correctly placed.

That summer I worked full-time at DBA. The Canada Dry warehouse/distribution center was finished enough to use by then, but DBA still had a bit to finish up on the fire alarm system. My typical workday that summer would find me working in the auto service shop, or maybe doing some maintenance on one of the several buildings DBA owned near downtown Denver and the State Capital Building. This day I was sent to work with the installing crew to help run wires inside the Canada Dry warehouse. Apparently so many of the installation crew were on vacation they were desperate for my help.

At the newly opened warehouse, I was impressed its size and how much pop there was under one roof. Forklifts were running from several loading docks unloading 40-foot trailers from the bottling plant, while other forklifts were hauling loads to trucks that would take the pop to stores, restaurants, and bars. I could have stood around watching the dance of the forklifts for a long time, but we had work to do.

In addition to all the activities shifting thousands of bottles and cans of pop, there was also ample office space. My job was to climb above the suspended ceiling and pull wire from a large spool down the offices' length. I was either walking on a top-plate of a wall or on a catwalk above the ceiling when I lost my balance and put a foot through one of the two-foot by four-foot ceiling tiles. It fell, landed on a desk before sliding the floor, and through the hole, I saw a very startled but unhurt secretary. Red-faced, I stared down at her and apologized. Back on the floor, I made sure to apologize again, and we agreed we both had been lucky that it was just the ceiling tile and not me that had fallen. That was the last time I was sent out with the installation crew.

Less than a year after breaking the ceiling tile, I was married to a very very pregnant Connie, and living in Seattle. I was hired as an apprentice machinist at Hallidie Machinery. Since the starting wage for an apprentice was 40% less than a journeyman machinist, and since Connie wasn't working, we were as poor as church mice. With rent to pay, the medical expenses for a soon-to-join-us baby, plus food, the very last thing we were going to spend money on was soda pop. As poor as we were, we were happy and looking forward to being parents.

As Connie neared her due date in July, Seattle experienced a heatwave with temperatures in the upper 90s. Being from Denver, we were used to temperatures like that, but with the added humidity of Seattle, Connie was miserable. And at work, I was too. At the time, Hallidie was housed in an old industrial building with limited cross ventilation and no air conditioning. Worse, machine motors and gears turning generated more heat. Many days, the temperature behind the metal lathe I normally operated was well over 100 degrees. Fortunately, there was an ancient Coke machine that resembled a chest freezer. When you'd open the top of the machine, all you'd see was the very top of bottles. After you deposited a dime, you moved pop bottle down slots to a particular location, a trap door would open, and you pulled out one bottle at a time. A dime was a lot of money to us back then, so when suffering in the heat of the machine shop, I usually stayed hydrated with free hot coffee, or lukewarm water from the bathroom sink. When I did spring for a Coke, and there was only Coke, as it cooled me down, I thought it was the best soda pop I had ever drunk.

The last time I had a soda was over two years ago when we were on a road trip. On that trip, Connie would occasionally buy me a small root beer or Dr. Pepper with lots of ice. Since I can only take small sips, I'd pour the soft drink into a thermos with a drinking spout. I'd sip on the soda all day long, guilt-

Old fashioned top-loading Coke machine.

free, knowing the calories would help me keep weight on, something most people with ALS have a hard time doing.

I'm lucky now if I can sip small sips of water. Any beverage like a soda pop is out. Not being much of a pop drinker anyway, I don't miss it. What I do miss is a morning cup of coffee, which I haven't been able to drink in over two years. But what I miss more than anything is being able to chug down a big cold ice-filled glass of what my good friend, Fr. Federer, called Adam's Ale – pure water.

As I enter my seventh year living with with bulbar onset ALS, I'm lucky to be alive. And I'm even more fortunate to have a brain full of many good memories, even if some are just about soda pop.

Postscript: After reading this, Fred told me the wire was a supervisory wire required by code. There is a device on the water main shutoff valve monitored 24/7 by a contractor or the fire department. That makes perfect sense. Say an arsonist wants to burn a building down. If they shut off the water main valve, the sprinkler system isn't going to work. Hence, the wire. And by code, the wire must be buried right alongside the water main.

Medical Aid in Dying

10 December 2020

Prescript: My friend who lives in Arizona and is part of a group called Arizona End-of-Life Options (AZELO) sent me an email in early December asking if I would write a letter in support of proposed legislation in his state. He and others in AZELO are supporting a bill called Medical Aid in Dying. Since I think people should have the right to Death with Dignity in all 50 states, I happily submitted the letter shown below.

To Whom it Concern,

December 11, 2020

There is an old saying, "Until you walk a mile in another person's shoes, you can't understand them." If I could talk, I would change that to say, "Until you ride a mile in my wheelchair, you won't understand." I have a terminal disease, and my neurologist told me when he was trying to figure out what I have, "We need to eliminate every possibility, because nothing is as bad as ALS." And when he and a whole host of medical personnel did eliminate everything else, Connie, my wife of 48 years, and I had to face the fact that I do have ALS.

Marcel LaPerriere

Facing ALS and knowing I will further decline is not scary to me. However, knowing I could linger in pain or a semiconscious state for months and months is darn frightening; much more terrifying than death. Of course, I want to extend my life as long as I can. However, I don't wish to live a life of endless pain and suffering. That is why I support Medical Aid in Dying legalization in all 50 states.

My wish is to one day fall asleep and never wake up. However, it would be comforting to know I had to right to medical aid in dying if I'm not lucky enough to die in my sleep.

Thank you for taking the time to read this letter, and thank you for considering death with dignity legalization.

Sincerely,

Marcel LaPerriere

Sitka, Alaska

Postscript: After I wrote a first draft of the letter that also expressed my concern about the financial burden end of life could place on Connie, I emailed it to my friend. He responded by asking me to exclude the part about finances, telling me that the opposition to the bill has fixated on that aspect. The opposition says the proposed legislation is all about cutting costs, putting saving money over life. I dropped that part of the letter. However, I think we, as people living with ALS, need to think about both emotional and financial burdens we put on our loved ones. Knowing that in the last six months of my life, medical costs could soar to over our net worth, concerns me deeply. The very last thing I want to do is force my wife into bankruptcy. So, I think that money should be part of the conversation. Shouldn't I have the right to die, knowing the inevitable could very well put my wife in a financial bind? I sure think so.

The Seven-Year Itch

26 December 2020

Supposedly, seven years into a romance, some people get an itch for a new partner. I'm now entering my seventh year living with ALS, and I never liked, let alone loved ALS. I've had the itch to get rid of it from day one. I sometimes even have the itch to trade ALS for any disease where there is at least a ray of hope to get better. One neurologist told me, "There isn't anything worse than ALS." So, I'd gladly give into the seven-year itch and trade this blasted disease for something more benign.

I'm lucky to be alive after seven years. When it comes to ALS, the seven-year itch must be modified. I long ago accepted that I have ALS, and that it isn't going to go away. So, as the seven-year itch gets itchier, I will continue to count my blessings, knowing it could be much worse.

One woman living with ALS recently posted on one of the ALS Facebook sites that her 2020 birthday present was finding out she also has breast cancer. Another young woman posted she just found out she has ALS at age 24. I've long ago lost track of how many posts I've read on Facebook where either the caregiver or the person with ALS is angry. Since I live in a beautiful town, in a beautiful state, in a very nice house with a woman I've loved for the past 48 years, I have nothing major to complain about, even if it is the year 2020.

Speaking of 2020, I scratch my head in wonder when I hear or read in the news about pandemic fatigue. I understand why, after all these months, people are tired of the restrictions. I, too, wish the pandemic would end. However, unlike the ALS I've been living with for seven years, the pandemic restrictions will end. Just like a broken bone will heal, social distancing, having to wear a mask, and home-confinement will soon end. The only way ALS is going to end for me is death. So, as much as I don't like what ALS has done to my body, things could be much worse. I'm not living in a war zone, I have a roof over my head, and I have a ton of things to live for.

I have the seven-year itch, and it's itching something terrible, but I'm lucky. Some of my ALS buddies have lost the use of their arms so they can't even scratch an itch. I can't walk or talk, but I can at least scratch an itch on my nose.

The seven-year itch won't go away, but it could be much worse. ALS sucks, but life is good.

Trust

4 January 2021

Daily we do things without giving them any thought. Take getting a glass of water from a tap. How do we know the water has just the right amount of chlorine in it, enough to kill harmful bacteria, but not enough to make us sick? We've not only trusted the technicians that oversee the machinery that adds the chlorine to our water, but we've trusted the science behind the chlorine to water ratio. And, we've trusted the government regulators to do their jobs of overseeing the water utility.

How about flipping on a light switch or plugging in your toaster. Do we know how our power is generated or how it gets to our house at just the correct voltage and frequency? Once again we are blindly trusting engineers, powerhouse operators, mechanics, linemen and women, and a whole host of others. And we are trusting government regulators who oversee and enforce standards set forward by the Federal Energy Regulatory Commission (FERC).

What about the gasoline we put in our automobiles? How do we know we are getting the octane we paid for or did we really get a whole gallon? We trust the science of refining the gas, and government regulators too. Government agencies like the EPA, FERC, the National Bureau of Standards, and others play a role in every gallon of gas we pump.

There are regulations that set standards for the food we eat, the medications we take, the soap we use, our toothpaste, and even the products' containers. What about the building materials in our houses? We trust the science, the engineering, and oh yea, those pesky government regulations. And I could fill an entire book on transportation, from public transportation to your car, to flying, to ferries. But I think you get the point I'm making about trust.

So, why don't people trust the science behind the coronavirus vaccine or listen to the experts regarding the warnings about Covid-19? Why won't many people trust Dr. Fauci, a man who has dedicated his life to infectious diseases? Sure, he and others have and will continue to make mistakes, but aren't mistakes how we learn? Plus, doesn't it make a lot more sense to trust people like Fauci over an unknown person posting on social media? I sure think so.

I can understand why there may be some hesitation over the Covid-19 vaccine. It was developed in record time, and using RNA is a new approach to vaccines. Scientists have been studying using RNA as a base for vaccines for over twenty years. This is the first time we have faced a worldwide pandemic in one hundred years. Fortunately, governments around the world recognized the world's economy depends on the vaccine. So, they funded Warp Speed and other fast-track developments. And, several pharmaceutical companies, universities, government regulators, and others stepped up to the plate and sped up the development of these very promising vaccines. At least in the United States, those mentioned above did this following standard protocols and without cutting necessary corners.

Just like I trust my local utilities and the government agencies that regulate them, I will be trusting the scientific foundations for the vaccine and the Food and Drug Administration. That's why I gladly rolled up my sleeve and got the first jab of the Pfizer vaccine, and in a couple of weeks, I'll once again get the second jab. I hope those that are reluctant to get the vaccine will give it further thought and consider all the things they take for granted.

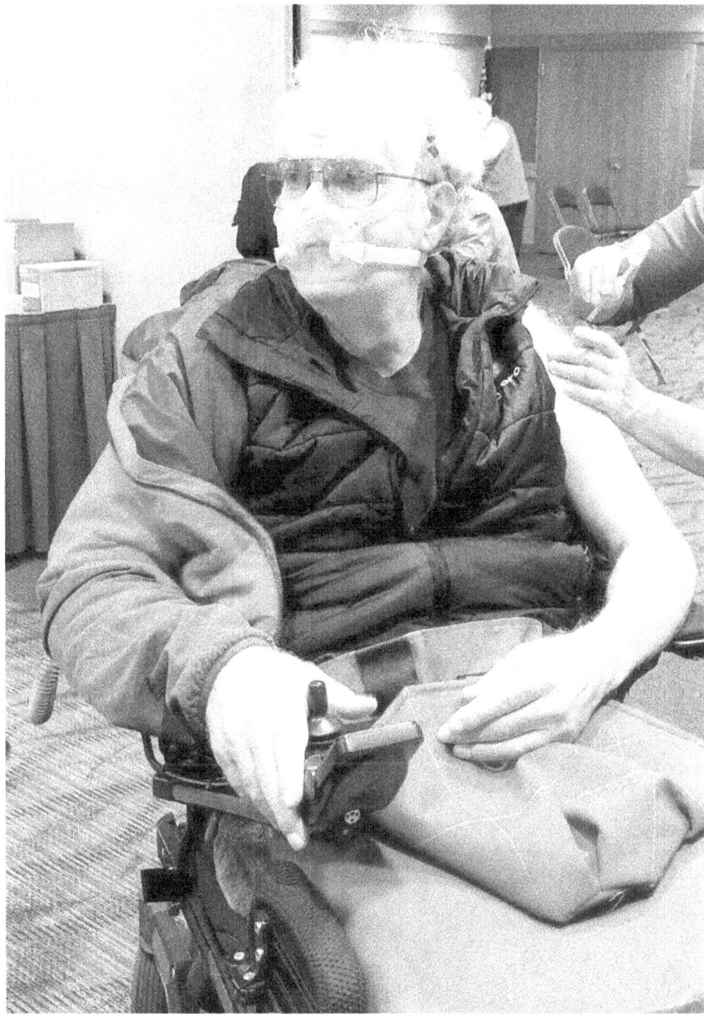

December 29, 2020. Getting my first of two Covid-19 shots. During the pandemic, I'd use my Trilogy noninvasive ventilator to protect myself from the virus when leaving the house.

Immortality

23 January 2021

It might seem like Michelangelo, born in 1475, Gustave Eiffel, designer and builder of the Eiffel Tower, born in 1832, and Mark Twain, born in 1835, have nothing in common. But they share something in common with many other great people, like Bach, Mozart, and even Anna McNeill Whistler, better known as Whistler's Mother. Their commonality is that they all gained a bit of immortality through their creativity. Further, Gustave Eiffel might have become famous for building the Eiffel Tower, but he couldn't have built it without all the craftsmen who did the actual work. Just like Michelangelo couldn't have painted the Sistine Chapel ceiling without the men who built the amazing cathedral. Nor could he have carved David without the quarrymen who quarried the marble. Just because the names of these craftsmen have been lost to time, they too earned a little immortality through their creativity and skills.

Through their evil deeds and destruction Adolf Hitler, Genghis Khan, and Joseph Stalin have also gained some immortality, as have the countless men and women who followed these monsters. Whereas Michelangelo, Twain, Eiffel, Bach, Mozart, and Whistler will be remembered for making the world a better place, the megalomaniacal autocrats Hitler, Khan, and Stalin leave a n eternal legacy of destruction and negativity associated with their names. Do the monsters of humanity deserve anything more from us than disdain? I don't think so.

We are the ones who decide how we are going to be remembered, and to some extent, what the world will look like when we are no longer here. Don't we all want a little immortality? I'll never leave an Eifel Tower or a David, and I'll never write a story half as good as Mark Twain. But shouldn't we all do what we can to leave the world a little better than when we entered it?

A few months ago, I met a young man who was in the first throes of ALS. In our short encounter, I could see that he was having a hard time dealing with the diagnosis. He was packed full of anger, and in his defense, how could he not be? However, he is in charge of dealing with that anger and how he will be remembered. Will he be remembered for that anger? Sadly, knowing he was charged with a domestic assault charge, I fear he is building the wrong kind of legacy. I frequently see posts ALS Facebook sites where someone asks how to deal with the anger and rage they see in their loved ones coping with ALS. One woman even posted these words, "I'm beginning to hate the man I once loved." We are the masters of our destiny.How we will be remembered.

Stephen Hawking, who lived with ALS for over fifty years, gained some immortality through his amazingly brilliant brain. Physicists and others will be reading Hawking's books and scientific papers for many years to come. Imagine if he had always been angry. Would he have lived as long as he did? And, look at what science and humanity would have lost if he had let bitterness rule his life.

How about Congressional Gold Medal winner Steve Gleason, the former NFL player.He will be remembered more for his work with Team Gleason than his football career. Isn't being remembered for our deeds as close as we can get to be immortal? I sure think so.

Take my father-in-law, George Durkop. If anyone had demons that could haunt him from his past, it would have been George. Imagine what it must have been like to watch your shipmates being eaten by sharks after the ship you were on was sunk by the Japanese during WWII. And before being rescued, he spent three days treading water after the aircraft carrier Gambier Bay was sunk during the Battle of Leyte Gulf. Yet after the war, he became a loving husband and father to four children. He also continued to serve his country, retiring from the Colorado Air National Guard as Chief Master Sergeant, the highest noncommissioned rank possible to achieve. I know his name will mostly be forgotten by history, but he gained a bit of immortality through his actions and deeds. Indeed, my son and his sons will keep George alive. And I hope that many generations from now, George's generation will be remembered for making the world a better place because of their sacrifices during WWII.

We are all mortal beings, and as close as we ever can become to being immortal is to leave a little bit of ourselves behind. Even if it is just good memories and a brighter future for those that come behind us. I hope for a brighter future, where humans live in harmony with the earth and all her creatures.

Goats and a Goofy Kid

4 February 2021

Lately, I've been dreaming about people from my past. It seems like as my ALS progresses, these dreams become more detailed and sharper. The clarity of these dreams often blurs the line between reality and dreams.

There have been many dreams about the guys I used to work with and several dreams about people who used to work for me. There was even a dream about a lady who was my mother's friend back in the '50s. But perhaps the most interesting and eccentric person I've recently dreamt about was a middle-aged lady named Mary Jo.

In the early '80s, we lived on Vashon Island and owned a machine shop located in our backyard. Even a small one-person backyard business occasionally needs to send formal business letters; letters to insurance companies, government agencies, and other companies. This was way before the Internet and personal computers, so professional-looking letters had to be typed using a typewriter. We didn't own a typewriter, but had seen an advertisement in the local newspaper for a professional typist who'd do typing by the page. As I re-call, the ad said $1.00 a page, which meant I could have a lot of typing done by a pro instead of buying a typewriter. That's how we met Mary Jo.

When she came to our house the first time to pick up a handwritten letter, we questioned our decision to hire out the typing instead of buying a type-writer. She was wearing bib overalls, and she smelt like goats. Since I grew up around cattle, horses, sheep, and even a few goats, I not only knew what a goat smells like, but I also knew that goat odor will overpower the aroma of other livestock. Goats stink. Though Mary Jo smelt like an old goat, she did an excellent typing job for a bargain price.

Eventually I dropped a typing job by her house. I was surprised when I rode my motorcycle down her long driveway at how nice her home looked. It was a much nicer house than I had suspected a goat lady would live in. It was no surprise, however, to see about a dozen goats wandering around her yard and climbing all over the large porch surrounding her ranch-style house.

Over the next two years, I learned not to be surprised when I heard some-thing new about Mary Jo. I found that she and her sister had grown up on Vashon, and had inherited the land from their father, who had been a prom-inent judge. And unlike Mary Jo, her sister had taken after their father and, became a well-respected judge. From time to time, I would see her sister men-tioned in a Seattle newspaper story about some high-profile criminal case. There weren't too many women judges at the time, so the articles always caught my eye.

Besides raising goats, Mary Jo made her living by typing depositions and court transcripts. I always wondered if those transcripts smelled as much like a goat as some of the letters she typed for us, especially after I went into her house. Most of the time, Mary Jo would bolt out of her house to gather the work before I had a chance to walk from my motorcycle to her door. But one nice summer day, she asked me in for a glass of iced tea, and I accepted. As we walked into her well-kept and clean living room, I could see a counter sepa-rated the kitchen from the dining room and living room. And on the dining table where we sat down to drink our tea was her typewriter and a couple of tape players; one a cassette player and the other a reel to reel. There was a couch in the living room with a goat sitting on it and goats coming and going from the house, just as pet dogs would. The house, and I'm sure everything in it, smelled like a goat.

Later, I wasn't surprised to see Mary Jo driving around the island with a goat or two in her pickup truck. Sometimes they'd be sitting in the back of the truck, but more than not, one or two goats would be sitting on the bench seat next to her. Once, when I ran into Mary Jo on the Vashon Ferry, I was sur-prised to see her wearing a respectable-looking dress. She told me she was on her way to testify in court. I wondered if anyone but me would smell the hint of goat that she was trying to conceal with perfume. Mary Jo was one heck of a character, but also one heck of a nice lady who just happened to have a soft spot for goats.

Now to another dream. I recently dreamed about a young man and stu-dent who worked for me when I ran the Maintenance Department at Sheldon Jackson College. To protect his and others identities, I'll call him Bob.

I first met Bob on his first day of college in his freshman year when he was sent to my office for an interview. He was to work two hours a day, five days a week, as a work-study student. Since I like mentoring kids, I approved his hir-ing, even though within about five minutes, I could see he would probably cost me more time and work than I'd gain from him. The purpose of the Federally funded Work-Study Program was to help pay for the student's education while the student got some work experience. As I suspected when I approved his em-ployment, Bob required much more supervision than the other kids.

Now back to my dream. As is often the case in dreams, people and places get scrambled. In this dream, my good friend, Roger from Ketchikan, was saying, "Bob sure is goofy," and continued, "Even if he is goofy, you can't help but like him." I agreed with Roger saying, "Yes, but he has a reason for being goofy. You see, he was raised by an uncle that might be goofier than he is."

This was when I woke up. I spent the better part of the next hour thinking about all the goofy things Bob had done in the two school years he worked for me. Though I could fill many pages with all the crazy and goofy things he did, I'll limit it to just a few stories. First, there was a call from campus security around 2:00 a.m. about Bob and a couple of other students. The first weekend that the students were on campus, they decided to test their new freedom by throwing a big party. As I cleared the sleep from my eyes, Frank, the security guard who worked for me, said Bob had to be rushed to the hospital because he had gotten so drunk. He had passed out and was convulsing. On a dare, Bob had chugged a fifth of whisky after already being staggering drunk on beer. Fortunately, after a night in the hospital, he recovered. After I gave him a long talking to, he said he had learned his lesson and swore off booze forever.

Bob was very good at talking about the uncle who was a plumber and had helped raise him. He would say, "That's not how my uncle does it," or "My uncle already taught me how to do that." One day, Bob learned a very painful lesson that his uncle didn't always know best.

One morning, working at my desk I heard the table saw in the woodshop start. Less than a minute later, I heard "Bang!" I ran back to the shop and saw that Bob was crosscutting a piece of wood against the table saw fence, and a chunk of wood had kicked back and had been tossed out of the saw. I repeated my lecture on table saw safety. "Bob, what have I already told you about crosscutting wood against the fence? Didn't I already say that rule number one is to keep your fingers clear of the blade, and rule number two is never, ever crosscut against the fence?" Bob answered, "My uncle does it all the time, and he taught me how to do it." I reminded him that we had a chop saw for crosscutting, and then admonished, "Don't ever do that again. I hope you have just seen how dangerous it is by your close call." With a nod of his head, I went back to my office.

After hearing the chop saw a couple of times, I once again listened to the table saw firing up. That got me back up from my desk. Bob wouldn't be that stupid, would he? Entering the shop, I heard the answer, "Bang," followed by a loud groan. I was just in time to see Bob hunch over moaning in pain. Bob had been stupid enough not to follow my safety instructions, and he hadn't learned from his mistake. An offcut had once again kicked back and was thrown with great force from the saw, hitting Bob right in the part of his anatomy that makes him a male. That incident and another one with a chainsaw forced me to ban him from ALL power tools. I didn't even allow him to use a cordless drill for several weeks.

Not long after the table saw incident, my boss, Fred, and I had an off-campus meeting to attend. Knowing I would miss Bob's scheduled work time, I asked my right-hand man, Jay, to meet Bob at the maintenance shop at his appointed work time. As we returned to the maintenance shop, Jay came running out the door. Before I even had a chance to turn off the truck engine, he said, "I saw the blood, I knew it had to be Bob, and I knew it had to be bad." Knowing the "Bob" was the goofy kid, Fred and I started to panic. There was a good chance Bob had hurt himself badly. Bob was cutting something with a razor knife he'd gotten from the wood shop a few minutes before his scheduled work time. The knife had slipped cut his leg. Jay had come into the maintenance a bit early to meet Bob, but he instead found a blood trail from the wood shop to the bathroom. Jay told Fred and me, "I made Bob unlock the door to the bathroom and let me in. He was trying to cover up the cut with paper towels, but I knew he needed stitches. Chuck took him to the hospital."

Chuck, a retired Presbyterian minister and a volunteer who worked for me running the office and doing light maintenance tasks, was also a great guy and a fantastic help to me in the first two years I worked at Sheldon Jackson

College. The near five-inch long cut in Bob's leg, required a fair number of stitches.

Since Bob was unquestionably the leader of the herd of goofy kids in the work-study program, though I have many more I could tell, here's one more.

Five historic buildings all built during 1910 and 1911 form the main Sheldon Jackson campus. One of the buildings, Whitmore, had a hedge in front and down part of one side of the building, and we used 120-volt power hedge-shears to keep the vegetation at bay. When one of the many volunteer gardeners told me that the GFCI outlet wasn't working, checking it out became a priority.

The GFCI had gone bad, and I asked Bob to help find the correct circuit breaker to turn off so I could replace the outlet. I showed Bob where the breakers were located and explained that there were up to a dozen breakers the outlet could be on. He was to shut one off and then wait for me to yell through an open window what to do next. When I had a meter hooked to the wires, I cried to Bob, "Turn off the first breaker." Since the power was still on, I yelled, "The power is still on. Reset that one and turn off the next one." When he got the correct breaker, I yelled, "That's it. Leave it off and come on out here." When he was outside, I proceed to change the outlet. As he walked towards me, I said to go back to what he'd been doing before our breaker job, and that when I was finished, I'd turn the power back on. Less than a minute later, zap, I got shocked. When Bob left me with a new GFCI outlet and bare wires in my hand, he went back into Whitmore and reset the breaker. As I let go of the wires, they hit the metal box and tripped the breaker. Bob was leaving Whitmore's from door as I ran towards it. Not being hurt, but more than a little pissed, I said, "Bob, why in the hell did you turn the power back on? I got a good shock and if I had been standing on wet ground, you could have killed me." Bob had no answer, and I once again learned what a goofy kid he really was.

As his first year in college progressed, I saw a little maturity settling on Bob, in part due to a young lady freshman I'll call Ashly. Unlike Bob, Ashly not only had her head on straight, but she seemed older than her years. They say opposites attract, and by the end of the school year, Bob and Ashly had fallen in love and had set a midsummer date for their wedding. And Bob asked me to be his best man, an honor I was happy to accept.

At the start of Bob and Ashly's sophomore year, they moved into a family housing apartment. Ashly must have been a tremendous influence on Bob; he wasn't anywhere near as goofy or as much work for me the second school year as he had been during the first. In fact, once he was living in family housing, he became the go-to guy when other students had a maintenance problem. He would often fix their problem, often before I even heard about it. Bob had become an asset rather than the significant liability he had been.

At the end of their sophomore year, Bob and Ashly transferred to a big university in Oregon, and I lost track of them. About five years after Sheldon Jackson College closed in 2007, I received an email from Bob telling me they had both landed well-paying jobs in the business world. Across many emails, Bob sent me several photos of their house and even a Google street view link of their neighborhood. Bob had come far from the goofy kid I'd first met. Again, I lost track of him for a few years and, the next time I heard anything about the young couple, they had gotten divorced. And per a couple of his old friends, Bob was suffering some serious mental health issues. Ashly had remarried and now has a child from her second marriage. I have no idea where Bob is today or how he is doing. The email address I had is no longer working.

I have no idea why so many people from my past are filling my dreams. Maybe my brain is sorting what should be tucked away in longtime memory and what should be trashed? The memories distract my mind from bad pain that keeps me awake while lying in bed for extended periods. And it's fun thinking about people like Mary Jo and a goofy kid named Bob. Whereas

Mary Jo had her kid goats, I often felt like I was herding kids, keep their mistakes to a minimum, and setting a good example for them.

Upon waking from a nap, I had dreamed I saw a poster of myself lying on my hospital-type bed, wrapped up in an electric blanket turned to the highest heat setting. A Trilogy noninvasive ventilator was also pumping heated air into my lungs. Printed on the poster were the words, "The warmings will continue until your body warms to normal temperature." I woke laughing, recognizing that the words were a pun on the tongue-in-cheek motivational poster that reads, "The beating will continue until morale improves." I woke up warm, laughing, and happy. Isn't that all most of us want? Especially when living with a devastating disease like ALS.

ALS sucks! However, life is good, especially when so many good people have touched that life. And dreaming of those people and the good memories I have of them is the frosting on the cake of life.

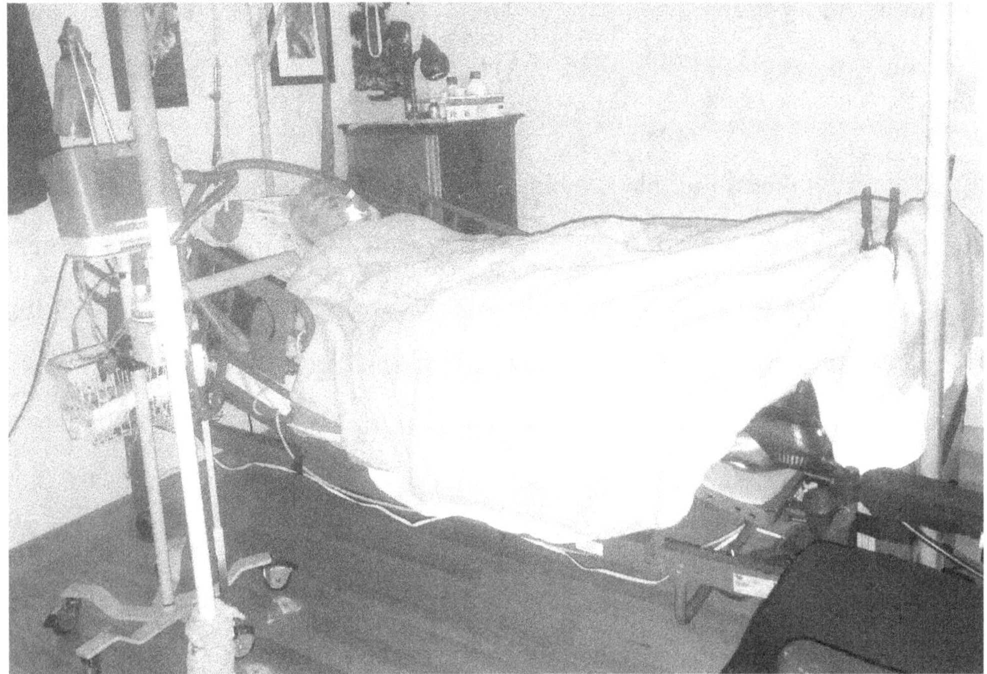

February 2021. Taking an afternoon nap and possibly dreaming about goats and goofy kids.

Give and Take

9 February 2021

I fatuously say ALS is the gift that keeps on giving. Were I a bit more serious, I'd say ALS is the crappy gift that keeps on taking. However, like most bad things, there are some good things about having ALS. Most people living with ALS would disagree with me, but for me, there are.

First, I've learned to be much more empathetic to others living with disabilities. Before I became disabled, like many non-disabled people, the disabled were mainly invisible to me. When I saw people in a wheelchairs or blind people with red-tipped white canes, I never gave much thought to how many obstacles those people must navigate daily. Things like a trash can in the middle of the sidewalk or the lack of curb cuts in the correct locations. And I was unquestionably guilty of pulling too far forward when parking, putting the bumper of my car halfway across a sidewalk. So I think it's good that ALS has given me more empathy.

Also, since ALS has made me much more emotional, I have gained empathy and compassion for both people and animals. Before ALS, sure, I'd get upset, but then I'd shrug off news about the misfortunes of others. Today, I can break down into tears over the news of a hurricane or some other natural disaster. And guaranteed, if I read about civilian casualties of war, it takes everything I have to not cry out in anguish.

I've also met, both virtually and in person, wonderful people from around the world that, indeed, I would have never met without ALS. Those people include dozens and dozens of people working in medical care. Most of those working in medicine are people with the biggest caring hearts of any people you'd ever meet. I feel lucky to have met them. And I can't forget all the people who have helped me put three books together about living with ALS. I already knew some of those folks, but without ALS, I would never have interacted with them to the extent I have.

Now to the taking. The ALS Monster robbed me of the ability to talk while at the same time making it hard to swallow. Then the beast robbed me of my ability to walk while at the same time limiting my ability to breathe. But possibly more painful are the less tangible losses of being able to hug my wife, kiss her, snuggle with her, or even hold hands. Plus, the loss of caring for myself or helping with daily chores. The latest thing ALS has given me is what the doctors call a neurogenic bladder. That means eight or nine times a day I must sit on the toilet for 20 to 40 minutes to drain my bladder. But even this has its good side; it gives me time to listen to a lot of podcasts.

The ALS Monster is a despicable bastard, one who will not be satisfied until it takes my life. However, I won't let it give me bitterness or self-pity. And I'll continue to count all the good things I wouldn't have experienced without it. If I could wish ALS away, I would. Until my last breath, I will count my blessings, knowing it could be worse. I'll even step out on a limb and thank

ALS for making me a better person all the while cursing it for making me a burden on others.

The Lack of Sleep Brought to You by the Letter "P"

7 March 2021

Last night, an hour after I went to bed, there was a knock on the door, which made our **p**upp**y** dog bark. Connie, already in her **p**ajamas, answered the door to find a **p**izza delivery **p**erson at the wrong **p**lace. I heard her tell the **p**izza delivery **p**erson the **p**roper **p**lace to deliver the **p**izza.

Then as I was drifting back to slee**p**, our **p**uppy dog had to go out to **p**oo.

Then I heard **p**eople talking outside. It ends u**p** there was a **p**arty two houses u**p** the street. Since Sitka now has 60 **p**ercent of its **p**opulation vaccinated against the virus that caused the **p**andemic, many **p**eople with **p**ent-up frustration caused by social distancing are currently attending many **p**arties.

Then the **p**uppy dog had to go outside once again, but this time to **p**ee. I lie in bed **p**ondering. Why can't the **p**uppy go outside to **p**ee and **p**oo at the same time?

An hour had **p**assed since the **p**izza delivery **p**erson was at the wrong **p**lace, and I was just about to fall aslee**p** when I heard the **p**ickup truck with no muffler **p**eel out on the **p**avement. Fortunately, the **p**ickup truck's owner recently told me a new muffler is expected soon at the **P**ost Office coming via **p**arcel **p**ost. I know, I'll be **p**retty **p**eeved if the **p**ickup truck owner **p**rocrastinates installing the new muffler once it arrives at the **P**ost Office.

I had just fallen aslee**p** when I heard the **p**ickup truck with no muffler that had **p**eeled out on the **p**avement returning.

Looking at the clock, I could tell I sle**p**t for an hour before the **p**ain of a full bladder forced me to get u**p** to **p**ee.

After I finished **p**eeing, I grabbed the floor-to-ceiling **p**ole, pulled myself u**p**, s**p**un 90 degrees, and **p**lopped down in my **p**ower wheelchair. After **p**owering u**p** next to my bed, I **p**arked the **p**ower wheelchair next to my bed. I then grabbed another floor-to-ceiling **p**ole, pulled myself u**p**, s**p**un, and **p**lopped down on my bed. After reattaching my noninvasive ventilator, Connie **p**ushed the button to turn the machine on that would **p**ush **p**ositive air into my lungs as I tried to slee**p**. She then **p**icked up my legs, gently **p**laced them on the bed, and then **p**ushed them into the center of the bed. After adjusting my **p**illow, I noted 45 minutes had **p**assed since I got u**p** to **p**ee.

After lying awake for the longest time, I fell aslee**p** for about an hour until the ever-**p**resent **p**ervasive **p**ain in my shoulder woke me u**p**.

For the remainder of the night, there was a **p**re**p**onderance of **p**ain that kept waking me u**p** every few minutes. Sometimes, it was the **p**ain from my back, sometimes, it was **p**ain from **p**ressure sores on my heels, and sometimes, it was just general **p**ain that kept me awake.

Then, like most early mornings, around 5:00 my calf muscles cram**p**ed u**p** in **p**ain. The **p**ain, of course, woke me u**p**, and again, like most mornings, I drifted in and out of slee**p** until I heard the Alaska Airlines **p**lane taking off as it **p**erpetually does each morning of the week around 6:00.

Through all the things that kept me from sleeping, I had to laugh at feeling like I was **p**art of the **P**BS **p**rogram, Sesame Street, where the letter **P** was the letter of the day. Or should, I say the letter of the night?

I just hope going forward, I can enjoy some **p**eaceful nights of **p**lacid slumber. However, I'm **p**assionate about being a **p**atient **p**erson living with ALS. I also know it's a **p**oignant fact in order to show **p**oliteness, one has to be **p**roud of one's tolerance **p**utting **up** with **p**ersistent adversity. After all, that is the **p**olite thing to do. **P**ossibly, that is what's meant when someone says, "Mind your **P**s & Qs?"

Thumbs and Reflections of Better Times

17 March 2021

Lately, as my hands continue to weaken, my thumbs have been incredibly sore, perhaps from gripping bars and poles as I transfer from my wheelchair to the toilet and from my wheelchair to my bed. And, opening child-proof caps on medications doesn't help. Even squeezing the pinch valve for my feeding tube can heighten the pain on an already sore thumb. Anyway, this got me thinking about thumbs and how important they are to us humans.

Like many things in life, we don't give much thought to our bodies or other things when they are working correctly. We jump into our automobiles, and if the engine starts, we drive away without giving any thought to how and why our cars or trucks work. Or we flip on a light switch without a second thought about what it takes to turn on the light. It's much the same with our bodies; until something doesn't work, we don't give it a second thought. With ALS, as more and more motor neurons die, we are forced to think about other failing parts of our bodies. For me, it's now the failure of my hands that I'm dealing with. And since my thumbs are sticking out like sore thumbs, and they have my full attention.

I'd give two thumbs down to thumb pain, especially when the throbbing of a thumb is forcing me to lie awake thinking about thumbs and how important they are. Since I can't talk, I often give the thumbs up or down sign when someone asks me how I'm doing. Or I might oscillate my hand with an extended thumb to answer, "so, so." And when Connie and I are streaming a documentary or a TV show, if something is unpleasant, I'll stick my thumb towards my mouth in a gagging gesture. I find myself making that gesture often when we watch other people's tastes in home decoration when watching shows like This Old House. Connie understands I don't like someone's taste in kitchen cabinets, flooring choice, or paint color just by the thumb to my mouth gesture. If a picture is worth a thousand words, a hand gesture using the thumb can be just as descriptive.

Speaking of descriptions about the use of thumbs, both in our written and spoken language, the thumb can be used as a shortcut, using fewer words than we otherwise might. If we say someone is all thumbs, the listener knows the person lacks coordination. Or if we say the guy sat on his thumbs all day, we know he has been lazy. And perhaps the most used of the thumb sayings: he stuck his thumb out for a ride. We know that person was hitchhiking.

The other night as I was lying awake trying to ignore the pain in my left thumb, I thought about my one and only real hitchhiking adventure. Growing up in a rural area, I'd hitchhike, knowing someone I knew would pick me up. When I was four or five, I'd take off walking the two miles to my friend Jimmy's house, and there was always better than a 50% chance a farmer or rancher I knew would give me a ride. And in high school, I'd sometimes hitchhike from my hometown, Sedalia, Colorado to Castle Rock. But between Sedalia and Castle Rock, there was an excellent chance someone I knew would give me a ride the minute I stuck my thumb out.

When I was in high school, I lived with my older brother, Fred, and his wife, Kay. Because I had worked every summer since I was seven years old and knowing after my senior year, there would be no such thing as a summer off, I decided not to work in the summer of 1971. By working several odd jobs, I had saved enough money to eek by. I planned to spend a lot of time hiking, climbing, and camping in the mountains. The only problem was I didn't have a driver's license, so I had to depend on others to get there. One morning, Fred drove me up to the mountains before he went to work, and after a couple of days hiking and camping on my own, I walked about ten miles to a payphone and called to be picked up.

Then after a couple of days back home, Kay offered me the use of her swaybacked horse, Bluff, to take me to the mountains to go camping. Let's just say I learned then that I'm no horseman. Fred noted that Bluff, aptly named, because the gelding was all bluff, pretended to buck and be cantankerous. This ruse would not have fooled anyone who was horse-wise, but Bluff sure bluffed me. A couple of hundred yards after climbing in the saddle, I found myself on the ground when I tried to ride him across the railroad tracks. After I dusted off the dirt, not wanting to admit defeat, I grabbed the reins and walked the very reluctant horse across the tracks. Once across the tracks, I remounted and rode the horse a couple of blocks to the main road through town.

As we approached the main road that we'd have to go down for a few blocks, Bluff tried to buck me off again. But, I prevailed, and it looked like everything was going okay until we reached a bridge over East Plumb Creek.Bluff made it clear I wasn't going to ride him over the bridge. Once again I dismounted and walked him over the bridge. Shortly after crossing the bridge, we turned down highway 105, better known as Perry Park Road, and all seemed to be going okay. Then something either spooked the horse, or I was once again bluffed by Bluff. Again I dismounted. As I led the reluctant horse, he saw some nice green grass alongside the road in the shade of some large walnut trees and I let him eat some grass; not an easy feat for a horse with a bridle and bit in his mouth. This was when I decided, riding Bluff to the mountain would be more trouble than it was worth. We turned around and walked the ¾ mile back home. After unsaddling the unenthusiastic horse, I told a surprised Kay that in the couple hours we'd been gone, we hadn't even made it a full mile from home. As I said, I'm no horseman.

Just a couple of days later my friend Steve came into the house ready to take off on a backpacking trip. Like teenagers often do, he had just argued with his parents and wanted a break from them. Steve would generally have had his car, but it had broken down. Therefore, we hatched a plan to take off on a hitchhiking adventure.

In the early 70s after Connie and I

We left for a few days were well be who knows! We're well equiped so don't worry! Send you a postcard from what ever jail we end up at. Tell steves parents if they call that we went to Pike Ntl Forst camping See you latter By now Marcel Berg Heil

Don't worry

The very sloppy note we hurriedly left for Fred and Kay. Note the phrase, Berg Heil, translated in English means, Good Climbing, or Mountains Hail. It was a phrase taught to me by my good friend, Fr. Federer.

were married, a truly kind Kay gave me a scrapbook of things she had saved from my high school years, which I still have. In it was the note we left her and Fred that Saturday, saying we had taken off. In the note, I tell Kay twice not to worry. Telling Kay not to worry is like dropping an ice cube on hot pavement and telling it not to melt. Or like cracking an egg into a sizzling hot pan and telling the egg not to fry. Kay just has one of the extra kind hearts, and she worries about anyone she cares about.

Initially, we had contemplated hopping a train, but we knew the northbound trains that transit through Sedalia went way too fast on the downhill descent into Denver. So that meant we'd have to hitchhike. A short walk soon had us standing on the side of US 85, Santa Fe Drive, thumbs out. Our first ride was probably from someone we knew, as I can't recall any of it. That driver let us off just a few miles down the highway where Santa Fe Drive intersects with Colorado 470. I have a vague recollection of sleeping that night in a large culvert, but perhaps we spread our sleeping bags out under a cottonwood tree? In the morning, we probably boiled water on my small Primus camp stove and had a cup of tea with a bowl of instant oatmeal. As the sun was coming up, we once again had our thumbs out, but this time it was in the westbound lane of Colorado 470. And nearly as quick as our thumbs were extended, a nice middle-aged man stopped and picked us up. Even better, he was heading to US 285 and beyond. That meant he could take us into the mountains.

As we drove westbound, he told us he was a minister and was on his way to his church in Conifer, where he would preach Sunday services. In the half-hour or so we rode with him, we talked about several things, including religion. He even asked us if we wanted to attend his service that day, but we wanted to get further into the mountains. He let us out, and within a minute we had our second ride of the day. That we got a ride so quickly didn't surprise us, but what did was who stopped. It was Fred and Kay. Kay had gotten worried and, figuratively speaking, found the needle in the haystack. We were on the third major highway since leaving home and about forty miles away from where we had first stuck our thumbs out. If they had been a minute or two on either side of the preacher dropping us off, they would have never found us. We had never told them where we were headed and, I don't think either of us ever learned how they guessed. Kay must have known Steve better than he possibly even knew himself, and figured out we were likely headed to Buena Vista. Kay also knew Steve had a crush on a girl named Jerrith, and she knew Jerrith's parents had a cabin there.

Jerrith was Reverend Hank's daughter, the minister at the church Steve and his family attended. Even though Jerrith was a year ahead of Steve and me, he still had a crush on her, and I think she thought Steve was okay too. Kay also knew Jerrith's younger brother, Jay, was a good friend of Steve's and mine. So Kay must have taken an educated guess and, knowing Rev. Hank and his family were on vacation at their cabin, that it was where we were heading. She and Fred got even luckier to find us standing on the roadside with our thumbs sticking out.

Nowadays, I have a lot of time to think about that magical summer between my junior and senior year in high school, the best summer of my youth. And with a thumb that throbs in pain, I need something to distract my mind. Try as I could, I couldn't remember the ride Fred and Kay gave us to Rev. Hank's cabin, but I remember the couple of weeks Steve and I spent around Buena Vista.

BUENA VISTA

As would be the case many times during Steve's life, the call to go fishing was greater than his calling to be around a female he was attracted to. Right after Fred and Kay dropped us at Rev. Hank's cabin, Steve, Jay, and I left with backpacks seeking seldom-fished streams in the Collegiate Peaks Wilderness Area. The first two days of the trip, it rained hard nonstop. While Steve braved the rain fishing nonstop, Jay and I kept a large campfire burning while standing under a tarp tied to large, blue spruce trees. Jay and I were happy each time Steve caught a fish, which we gladly cleaned before cooking it on the open fire.

I was always much happier climbing peaks than fishing, so after a couple of days of rain, we hiked deeper into the wilderness. While Steve and Jay fished, I started bagging peaks, sometimes going from one summit down a ridge and up the next. I'd be back in camp in the late afternoon, where there was always a trout dinner ready to be cooked and eaten. One day we got up early and hiked into a small lake at the base of Mt. Yale. Since it was about noon when we set up camp, I figured I'd have plenty of time to hike up Yale. While my two friends fished, unknown to me, I'd soon experience a somewhat rare phenomenon. Bidding my friends farewell, and with an extra-light pack on my back, I headed up the mountain.

As a teenager, no one I ever met could keep up with me hiking. This was even true at high elevations. So, hiking by myself, I was making good time up the ridge heading to the summit. I was, without doubt, looking forward to a candy bar as a reward when I reached the summit. However, the reward of reaching the summit didn't happen that day. Just a few hundred feet ahead within sight of the summit every sense in my body went into overload. I'm not sure if I was fascinated or totally terrified of what was happening all around me. I don't know if I first saw, heard, felt, smelled, or even tasted the luminescent plasma known as Saint Elmo's Fire. But every sense in my body was working overtime, detecting the incredible energy of nature. As the alpine plants' tips glowed blue, I heard a buzzing, and smelled ozone in the air. Indeed, the closest way to describe what I was feeling is that my entire body felt as if it was electrically charged; something like the feeling you sometimes get just a millisecond before a static-electric shock. Whether the feeling was real or psychosomatic I don't know. It was a phenomenal experience, like nothing

I'd experienced up to then or since. I understood that I was witnessing a phenomenon that few people have or will experience.

Fascinating as it was, I knew I'd best get the hell out of Dodge. Though I knew little about the luminescence I witnessed, I knew it meant lighting could strike soon. And the last place I wanted to be with an aluminum-frame pack on my back holding a long ice ax was standing near a Rocky Mountain summit. The ridge that I had come up was now starting to glow, and as lightning flashed all around me on every peak in view, I saw a snowfield that led to a gully heading down the west face of the mountain. I took off running, and as soon as I hit the snow, I went into a standing glissade, sometimes running and sometimes skiing on my boots. When the slope got steep enough, I sat and glissaded down the face at breakneck speed. After I had descended a couple of thousand feet, I felt safe enough to slow my decent and reflect on what I'd witnessed.

That afternoon I was glad to be back in camp with my two friends, sharing yet another meal of freshly caught trout and telling them about my adventure on Mt. Yale. Less than 24 hours after my rapid descent, all three of us stood on its summit. We surveyed where we had come from and where we planned to go the next day from our lofty no-St. Elmo's Fire-today perch.

The following day, we hiked over a pass that took us way above tree line, and once over the pass, being silly teenagers, we joyfully ran down the other side. Running, whooping and hollering, our voices echoed off the steep mountains, and we tried to outdo each other with our yells. And then we broke into screaming at each other in French, or what we assumed a Frenchman would sound like. "Nous sommes des hommes de montagne," one of us yelled. Followed by, "Oui, nous sommes hommes de montagne." We continued, sometimes somewhat knowing from our French classes what we were saying, and sometimes not. "On adore les montagnes!"

We kept being silly and saw some signs of past gold prospecting from the 1860s. There were many glory holes, both vertical and a few horizontal shafts, that we stopped to explore. Then, off in the distance, further down the valley, we saw some rustic old buildings amongst old mine tailings about a mile away. These sparked our excitement, and we sped up our descent, all the while yelling, "Nous sommes des hommes de montagne," and other nonsense.

Since we'd entered the Collegiate Peaks Wilderness Area, we hadn't seen another soul. So we were surprised, and because of our silliness, a bit embarrassed, when we saw a man coming out from one of the dilapidated buildings. Red-faced, we said hello and introduced ourselves. He asked about or yelling, and to our surprise, he even recognized we had been screaming in French. I can only assume, especially when he heard my name, he was somewhat confused when we had to admit we were being silly and only knew some schoolroom French words. The man we met was extra friendly and even graciously offered us first lunch and later dinner; a welcome change from oatmeal and trout.

The man was a college professor and had picked the solitude of the wilderness to spend his summer writing a book. Unfortunately, I don't remember his name, where he taught, or what he was writing about. The buildings and the mine were part of an inholding within the wilderness, being an old, patented gold mining claim. The mine owners had permitted the professor to spend the summer in one of the old cabins. After giving us a tour of the old buildings, which were full of old machinery that I found fascinating, he told us the mines were too dangerous to enter. Closer to our homes, Steve and I had already explored dozens of old mines, but not wanting to go against what our host was telling us, we didn't push the issue.

While eating lunch in the professor's cabin, we talked about what a task it would have been in the 19th century to haul large machinery and supplies into the mine. After all, even in 1971, we were about twenty miles from the nearest road, so what would it have been like a hundred years before we were there?

After camping outside the cabin, we got up to the glorious smell of coffee, and for the third time in a row, the professor asked us to join him for a meal. We, of course, said yes, which I think made him happy. He had already told us he hadn't seen anyone in about a month, so I assume he was starving for human contact, even if it was three goofy teenage boys. He served us flapjacks with fake maple syrup but no butter, which we understood. Everything he needed had been hauled in by mules and horses, so something like butter might have been too costly a luxury. After breakfast and a few cups of coffee, we bid the professor goodbye and followed a valley down the mountain, that soon had us back in a beautiful forest.

Having spent a lot of time in the Colorado mountains, we knew that it could snow any month of the year. And as we hiked through the forest, snow began to fall. All three of us were thrilled at the snow, even when it got close to the top of my ankle-high mountaineering boots. Lunchtime probably found us sheltered under a tree eating peanut butter and a chocolate bar which we washed down with a cup of hot tea. It wasn't a big hassle to dig out my stove and heat a Billy can of hot water for tea. Steve and I would have preferred steaming hot coffee, but tea bags are much easier to pack. Hence, the tea. Ironically, I always used an old empty coffee can as my Billy can.

In the early afternoon, we first assumed that the well-maintained cabin we saw in the distance was at a road. To our surprise, it and another old rickety cabin sat in the woods near a stream, but with no road in sight. More surprising was the neatly painted sign nailed to the cabin wall to one side of the front door, "Welcome. Use but don't abuse." On the dining table next to the open fireplace, was a guest book and some rules, the gist of which was the same tenor as the welcome sign. Even with the welcome sign, I felt a bit uncomfortable using the cabin, but my two friends overruled me, and soon we had a roaring fire going in the fireplace.

We all agreed if we were going to use the cabin, we should cut some firewood. Using all hand-tools and going deep into the forest to find deadwood, three teen boys in good shape can cut a lot of wood in short order. In just two or three hours we had the attached woodshed filled with split firewood. With our one night's rent paid in firewood, I didn't feel too guilty unrolling my sleeping bag on the floor not far from the fireplace. But I think Steve and Jay rolled their sleeping bags on beds.

After a good night's sleep, we swept the cabin floor, washed the tabletop, and tidied up the cabin, leaving it as good or better than we had found it. In typical Colorado fashion, in contrast to the previous day with snow, it was a glorious day as we left the cabin. We hiked another five or six miles and found ourselves out on the road far from where we had entered the wilderness. Jay called his dad from a payphone we found and he drove to pick us up. Our ten days or so in the Collegiate Peaks Wilderness Area had come to an end, but my summer of adventure was far from over.

Family details. By the end of the summer we spent in the company of Reverend Hank's son, Jay, the kind preacher had already married my sister, Andree, to her first husband, Pat. And just five short years later, he married Steve to my younger sister, Chelly. Possibly, even more interesting, when Reverend Hank was in his mid-90s, he married Andree's granddaughter, Justine.

THE TETONS

Besides sore thumbs, as my ALS progresses, it seems like a painful neck, back, or some other joint pain deprives me of sleep. As much as I want and need sleep, I'm happy that my mind and memory still seem to be intact. On subsequent nights, I recalled that one summer of fun and beyond.

After returning home, my friends, Stratton (Strat) and his brother, William (Bill), and I headed to the Tetons for a couple of weeks. Since Strat had a dri-

The Mercury Parklane that took us from Colorado to the Tetons.

ver's license but not a car, we took one of my brother Fred's cars. The car was a luxury Mercury Parklane, with the signature reverse back window, electric everything; windows, seats, and even an antenna that lowered and raised with a motor. Being a jerk and a vindictive man, Fred's boss, Stewart, had sold the car to Fred for $100.00 rather than give it to his ex-wife in a divorce settlement. As I understand, the divorce papers said his wife was to get the Mercury, but instead of the relatively new car, he gave her an old piece of junk he got from a junkyard.

Since there wasn't any speed limit in large sections of Wyoming in the early 70s, it's a miracle that the Parklane didn't kill us three boys. One time we came over a hill going close to 100 miles per hour, and standing right in the road were a dozen or so wild horses. Strat slammed on the brakes, and as the car laid a swerving line of rubber, horses scattered in all directions. I don't know how we didn't hit one, or worse, several horses. Strat had good reflexes. After that close call, sweat pouring from our brows, we decided to slow down to a somewhat more reasonable speed. A valuable lesson was learned. Just because you can legally drive like a maniac doesn't mean you should.

During the previous summer of 1970, Bill, Strat, and I had attended the Exum School of Mountaineering to learn the basics of rock climbing. In '71, we focused schooling on advanced rock climbing, ice climbing, and glacier res-

Summer 1970. Bill topping out on a short climb.

cue techniques. After a week of schooling, we paid a guide, first to take us up the Exum Route on the Grand Teton, and then Southwest Ridge of Symmetry Spire, a 7-pitch climb. We figured that climbing with a guide would increase our climbing skills, which it did. We then spent a couple of days climbing easier, one and two pitch climbs on the Guide's Wall.

Being poor, we had to cut expenses every way we could. That meant both summers Strat, Bill, and I were in the Tetons, we didn't want to spend money camping in the National Park campgrounds. So, the first summer we were there, we found a side road that took off from the main road and ran along the southwest shore of Jackson Lake. A couple of miles down that road and a half-mile walk through the woods took us to the lakeshore, where we found a fantastic spot to set up two tents. It was not legal to camp within the park if you're not camping in a campground. That didn't stop us; we'd just have to be careful. First, we had to find a place to park the car where there was a low chance of a Ranger spotting it. Then, as much as we wanted to set up our tents right on the beach of the lake, we knew we couldn't. And what fun is it to camp without having a campfire? That just meant we had to limit our fires to after dark, and we'd have to keep them small, no easy task for teenage boys. All that must have worked because two summers in a row, we didn't get caught illegally camping.

Since nowadays, I rarely sleep much over an hour without waking up, I have a lot of time to reflect back to better days. It would get really hot most afternoons in the Tetons and how we'd cool off by swimming in Jackson Lake. This is where it was darn handy to have our camp close to the lake, just far enough from the shore so the tents couldn't be easily seen, but an easy walk in bare feet. At first, we swam only a couple of hundred feet from shore. But being adventurous teens, as each day passed, we got braver and braver, swimming further from shore each afternoon. One day we decided to swim from our camp a good mile out to a small island.

Summer 1971. Our Exum School Guide leads us up Symmetry Spire.

Whereas Bill and I tended to use the breaststroke or freestyle stroke primarily, Strat tended to use a backstroke which gave Bill and me a few laughs. Bill and I'd look over to see Strat swimming in the wrong direction or in circles, and get him back on heading. After a good half-hour of swimming, we stepped onto the island, and after a few minutes sitting in the low evening sun, headed back to camp. Knowing the sun would be setting soon, we decided we best stick together. That way, Bill and I could keep Strat swimming in the right direction.

When I've told this story to others, I've sometimes been asked, "Weren't you afraid to swim so far out into the lake?" I can truthfully say, "No." Even if we lacked style, all three of us were strong swimmers. However, when we were about halfway back to our camp, we saw a BIG boat heading fast right towards us. We all started waving our arms, and at the last second the boat turned and motored past us, missing us by just a few feet. Just because we missed being physically hurt, doesn't mean we got off scot-free. The skipper of the boat turned around and gave us a verbal lashing for being so stupid. He, of course, was right, and that ended our long-distance swimming.

We'd planned on leaving the Tetons shortly after the swimming close call, by way of a couple days backpacking in the Wind River Range. Those plans quickly changed when we knocked a hole in the Parklane's oil pan. The road that ran along the southwest side of Jackson Lake was more of a four-wheel-drive road than anything the Parklane should be driving on. For two summers in a row, Strat had skillfully navigated the road, avoiding the large ruts and anyplace the Parklane could high center. The last day we drove that road, Strat hit a rut six inches to one side of where he'd driven the road dozens of times before. With a big crunch, the Parklane slid into the rut, and the car's oil pan landed right on top of a pointy rock. Fortunately, Strat was able to back off the rock and out of the ditch before the oil pan ran dry.

Broken down over 500-miles from home and with little money isn't a good place to find oneself in. We did have a complete toolbox of tools, and I was an okay auto mechanic. Strat, empty backpack clad and feeling guilty about the mishap, walked to the main road to hitch a ride into Jackson Hole where he planned on buying several quarts of oil. Meanwhile, Bill and I jacked up the car and found large rocks to stick under the two front tires. I then slid under the car and got my first good look at the hole. At first glance, the half-inch wide and three-inch long hole didn't look like it could be repaired. I feared we have to buy a new oil pan. But I soon saw a possible temporary fix, so I started removing it.

On the Parklane, unlike many cars, nothing major interfered with the pan dropping right off. Except in our case. The front axle barely prevented the pan from dropping free. Lifting the engine just an inch would do the trick. So I removed the engine mount bolts, and with a jack under the pulley mounted to the crankshaft, Bill and I jacked the engine up just enough to remove the pan. Using a large rock as an anvil, I was able to pound the metal so that the half-inch wide hole was now almost closed. I hoped that would reduce the gush to into a steady drip. I then remounted the pan. Fortunately, the cork gasket was still attached to the pan wasn't hurt when I removed it from the engine.

When Strat got back with the oil, we refilled the engine and drove to Jackson Hole in search of a welding shop that could weld the pan. I planned to remove the pan once again, have it welded, and then we could still head to the Wind Rivers. But the welding shop owner told us the metal was too thin and un-weldable. Thus, we headed home, with no detour through the Wind Rivers. (Later when we got home, I proved him wrong when I welded the crack in the pan shut with Fred's inexpensive buzz-box welder.)

To console ourselves after the disappointment of missing the Wind Rivers, we sprung for burgers, fries, and milkshakes. Funny, all these years later, I recall how good our meal was, and, if it is still there, I could easily navigate to the drive-in where we ate. It was just that good.

After eating, we picked up a case of heavy-weight oil and several cans of STP, which had the consistency of cold honey at room temperature. We hoped the thick STP and the heavy-weight oil would, slow the leak enough to get home. Every 20 minutes, we pulled over and add at least a quart of oil and sometimes another can of STP. Today, I'd be terrified of the thought of leaking a stream of oil all the way from the Tetons to our home in Sedalia, Colorado, but at the time, we didn't give it a second thought.

Thinking of the trip to the Tetons and the Parklane, I also thought about what fun that car was. Shortly after we returned home from the Tetons, I got my driver's license. I'd drive the car from time to time, and all my friends thought the reverse back window that lowered was pretty cool. Kay would have been terrified to know this, but at one time or the other, everyone who rode in the car would lower that window, climb out and sit on the trunk facing forward with legs still inside. We'd then rest our arms on the roof of the vehicle, much like one rests one's arms on a table. We all thought it was darn fun to feel the wind blowing through our hair, much like one feels when riding a motorcycle. The difference was three guys could sit side by side, grinning and shooting the breeze as the breeze flowed over the car's roof. As much as I drove around with friends hanging out of the back window, it was this side of a miracle that I never got pulled over.

I also thought about the fire that Fred experienced driving the Parklane. He was driving home from work one day down Happy Canyon Road and the car suddenly had smoke pouring out from under the hood. Not a very happy day driving on Happy Canyon Road.

Ford, in not one of its better ideas, ran the large charging wire that runs from the alternator to the battery a few feet inside the car's wiring harness. For some unknown reason, the large wire heated up, and the insulation melted off that wire. That caused most of the wires that were bundled together in the harness to melt and catch on fire. Because of where the large wire from the alternator melted, none of the other wires were protected by fuses. So literally, every wire in the car caught fire. Fortunately, as soon as he saw smoke, Fred shut the engine off, and that stopped the whole vehicle from being engulfed in flames. Since everything in the Parklane was electric, Fred and I spent many hours rewiring the entire car. And shortly after we got the car rewired, Fred sold it to a friend.

MOUNTAIN CABIN

Over the next few nights, while I contemplated how living with ALS isn't much fun, I also thought back to the rest of the summer fifty years ago. Being mid-August, summer was waning, and it was nearing time to go back to school. Jerry, another friend called and asked if I wanted to attend an overnight party at a mountain cabin where our mutual friend, Scott, and his cute younger sister, Connie, were staying. Yes, that Connie. The gal I married. Of course, I said yes.

Connie, Scott, and their/our friends were staying at the Durkop family cabin, sans parents. This gave the kids a bit of freedom and gave their parents a preview of what an empty nest life would be like. The cabin had a large living room with a rock fireplace and kitchen/dining room attached. About a dozen of our friends from high school were already there when we arrived. All the kids had been in drama classes and many after-school plays; there was no doubt we were the drama freaks. There was the brainiac, Leah, who would shortly be awarded a Boettcher Scholarship. Leah was mostly likely there with her best friend Ann, the foulest-mouthed girl I ever knew, and the polar opposite of Leah when it came to scholastics and most everything else except their love of the theater. Also there was Connie's best friend Laura, who came from a wealthy, but not uppity family. Harold, a good friend of mine, and the star in most of our productions was already there. As was Bob, a big awkward kid who'd often trip on his own feet. Since he lived near Harold, they probably came together.

Three or four of those kids had probably crammed themselves into Harold's VW bug to get there. Those days, few kids owned their own cars and it was before the seatbelt laws. Harold's bug frequently overflowed with kids sitting on each other's laps. One short ride of just over a mile from the high school to Moore's Restaurant, the local hamburger joint, we crammed ten kids into Harold's bug, built for four. On that trip, Connie, being the smallest, laid in the space between the backseat and the back window!

I had started my summer trying to be a cowboy, riding Bluff, and then had spent time with Steve, who could have safely been called a redneck. Then the trip to the Tetons with my two friends, Strat and Bill, who excelled in academics. And I was finishing off the summer, perhaps where I felt the most at home, was with my fellow drama freaks. They ran the gamut; cowboys, hippies, rednecks, and academics. And the drama kids knew how to have fun without alcohol, or worse, drugs, something many of my cowboy and redneck friends struggled to do.

As a teenager, who didn't drink, smoke dope or even cigarettes, I loved attending the drama freak parties where silliness always ruled. We'd often reenact the plays we had been in, sometimes with a twist on the plot. Since Harold had sung the lead in the *Man of la Mancha*, the *Fantasticks*, *Fiddler on the Roof*, and a few others, he was often the butt of a few jokes when we made up parody songs. Harold always took the jokes well, and join in with his marvelous baritone voice. If we were lucky, Harold, would dig out his 12-string acoustic guitar, and play a few of the many tunes he knew by heart. My popularity, at this or most any party, came with the dozens of fresh-baked cookies baked by Kay my sister-in-law. We drama freaks proved it possible to have a ton of fun without drinking or smoking pot.

When I saw Connie, I was surprised to see her wearing a neck brace. That's when she and Scott told us about the accident they'd been in. It seems Scott was spending the summer helping our drama teacher, Mr. Larson, build a house not far from the cabin he and Connie were staying in, and they were driving the Larson's Jeep to and from the cabin to the construction site. One evening after work, with Scott behind the wheel and Connie riding in the passenger seat, they drove off a twisty mountain road and flipped the Jeep onto its side and then over on its top. This was before seatbelts were standard in vehicles, and in this case, it's a good thing. Because the Jeep didn't have a roll-bar, and the ragtop was down at the time, if they hadn't been thrown clear, they would have been crushed under the Jeep.

Scott had been drinking a cream soda, and as he tipped his head back to let the soda flow into his mouth, he hit a small curb that directed water into a culvert. Fortunately, he was driving the speed limit, but unfortunately, he was driving a Jeep. At the time, the Ford Bronco and the Jeep had a nasty habit of flipping over when they hit a bump that other vehicles would bounce right over. Here is what would happen. The light vehicles, with little weight on the front wheels, would turn sharp enough that even at low speeds, they would flip. Whereas other four-wheel-drive vehicles with a larger turning radius would turn, the Jeep and Bronco would roll over instead. After killing several people, both Ford and Jeep lost major liability lawsuits over their less-than-stable vehicles. I tell you this to partially exonerate Scott from blame.

With the Jeep driving down the road one minute and a split-second later rolling over, Connie could not have seen it coming. While Scott was driving and drinking a soda, she, sitting cross-legged, was looking down as she hemmed the legs of new pants she had just purchased that very day.

Connie told us about her trip in the ambulance to the hospital and two somewhat funny stories. Apparently she had been walking around much of that summer barefooted, which meant her feet had developed some hearty cal-

Connie shortly after the accident.

luses. And to add to her less than feminine feet, a few days before the accident, she had walked barefoot in uncured cement she and Scott had helped the Larsons pour for their garage floor. The combination left her feet looking like she was a Himalayan Sherpa and not a petit Colorado teenage girl. Connie told us her feet were the horror of more than one nurse, many of whom thought they had been injured in the accident. More than one nurse kept covering Connie's feet as she laid on the gurney.

The other story Connie told us involved her parents and showed she had a concussion. When told her parents had arrived, Connie said, "They are not exactly my favorite parents," which was far from true.

As Connie and Scott told us the story, I found myself with a pit in my stomach, running "what-ifs" in my mind. What if they'd been wearing seatbelts? What if Connie had been tossed through the windshield? What if the Jeep had landed on her? Possibly, for the first time in my life, I found myself fearing for someone I obviously had deep feelings for. Gosh, was I already falling in love with the gal I'd spend the rest of my life with? No one could have answered that question. Nor could anyone have guessed that two years later Connie and I'd be married and living in Seattle with our infant son.

Fifty years later, I sometimes marvel at how I can remember so many details from that magical summer. If you asked me what dinner Connie pureed for me yesterday, I'd be hard-pressed to recall what it was. Even what we did on vacation ten years ago would be a real challenge. Yet, somehow, I can clearly remember much of my childhood. Perhaps, because, as humans, our brains are still developing into our mid-twenties. Plus, just like a computer, we chose what to keep in memory and what to delete. Perhaps even our dreams help us preserve our memories.

Nowadays, I sleep like crap, which gives me a lot of time to remember my youth, some good times and some not-so-good times. Today is Saint Patrick's Day, which marks the 61st anniversary of my mother's death. Her death, when I was seven years old, changed the trajectory of my life. My father felt his kids were nothing more than his personal slaves. Before her death, being a good mother, she kept our father from working us to death. She also kept him from beating us when he wasn't happy with the work we had done. After her death, our father and his second wife looked at us kids as just another means to achieve what they wanted. That's how I found myself doing all sorts of jobs as a kid that would typically, at least in the Western world, be done by adults.

As I mentioned, the summer of 1971 was the only summer I didn't work during my childhood. And some of those jobs now seem unreal for a kid. One job was working as a hod carrier for both my dad and a stonemason he hired. At the age of about nine I helped my dad with the blockwork to build a massive three-story high fireplace with two fireboxes. Then I helped the hired stonemason cover the blockwork with cut stone. I mixed endless batches of mortar before carrying it in buckets to my dad or the stonemason. It was my job to keep both men supplied with either cinderblock or stone. I also did a fair amount of the pointing, fairing out the mortar between block or stone, and many hours cleaning the tools, often while my dad relaxed, enjoying a glass of wine or a cold beer.

I was about ten when I helped a cowboy who owned a one-eyed horse named Domino re-fence my father's and my uncle Bob's adjacent land. The old rusty barbwire fences were in bad repair with rotting scrub oak and pitch pine fence posts. The fence wasn't worth repairing. Plus, a new survey found that the about the ½-mile-long backline was off. That meant we moved the fence in my dad's and uncle's favor about five feet to the east. (I later found out that when my dad and uncle sold their land, the original fence had been in the right place after all. When they sold, the fence was once again moved. But for several years, they got free grazing use of a five-foot-wide swath of land a half-mile long.) Fencing the backline and four sides of the 40-some acres, plus building a new fence between my dad's and my uncle's land, took the old cowboy and me a couple of months. As hard as the work was, it was kind of fun. The old cowboy treated me well, and while we worked, he told me many great stories. After we finished building the fence, I used a hand-bow saw to cut the hundreds of old fenceposts into firewood.

By the time I left home at the age of fourteen, I had worked helping my father with all phases of building, including wiring and plumbing. Plus, every summer I had, mostly by myself, taken care of a couple of acres of evergreen nursery where we grew ponderosa pine, Colorado blue spruce, and juniper. My older brothers, Jay and Fred, had helped plant the hundreds of trees, and when they left home, it fell on me to weed, water, and fertilizer the trees my dad sold each fall. As trees were sold, more saplings were planted, and it was my job to care for them, as well. There was a good acre of lawn and associated landscaping to take care of in between other work. And, if that wasn't enough, there were always animals to feed, water, and groom. While my sister, Andree, was kept busy doing endless housework and taking care of infant and toddler step-siblings, I always had outside work to do.

I even worked the two summers I lived with my aunt and uncle. I'd get up at 4:30 a.m. and deliver two large routes of the Rocky Mountain News, which would take me a couple of hours. Then, most days, by 9:00 a.m., I'd start mowing lawns in the neighborhood. And how many Americans can say they worked for room and board, plus a token stipend during the summer between their freshman and sophomore years in high school? That summer I lived and worked about 50 hours per week at a Catholic retreat house.

See why that one summer of fun during my teenage years was special to me and why I have spent many sleepless nights thinking about it? As ALS keeps taking from me, I genuinely take comfort in all my good memories. Besides thinking of all the good times, I continue to think about all I owe my brother, Fred, for saving my sisters, Chelly and Andree and me from the hell we lived in for seven years. Plus, I've thought about how Fred and Kay were kind enough to grant me one summer where I could be a kid. My father wouldn't have but my brother and his wife did. And I can never forget that my life, even living with ALS, is much brighter because of the woman I fell in love with all those years ago.

I started this essay by talking about thumbs and how important they are for us humans. Almost nothing I've done in my life would have been possible without my hands and thumbs. Now ALS is robbing me of the use of them and the rest of my fingers, too. For that, while I still can, I give two thumbs down to ALS and what it has robbed from me. But I give two thumbs up to life and great memories. I also give two thumbs up to that one summer that I've dedicated so much time thinking about these last few nights.

Lou Gehrig Day and Nostalgia

26 April 2021

The motor neuron disease we call amyotropic lateral sclerosis (ALS) is often sadly called Lou Gehrig's Disease, sadly because Lou Gehrig, instead of being remembered for being one the best first basemen in major league baseball, is remembered for this devastating disease. Sometimes people have asked me or told me I have Lou Gehrig's Disease. If I could talk, I'd yell, "I have ALS, a type of motor neuron disease, and not Lou Gehrig's Disease." I feel bad for Mr. Gehrig, just as I would feel bad if ALS had been named after Stephen Hawkings, perhaps the most famous person who had the misfortune to live with ALS. Why should anyone have such a devastating disease named after them? I hate it and don't think it's fair to anyone's legacy.

Unlike most Americans, I'd rather watch paint dry or grass grow than watch professional baseball on TV. However, it's great, after a grassroots movement lead by a handful of pALS, and cALS, that major league baseball designated June second, in perpetuity, as Lou Gehrig Day. The day will help raise awareness of ALS, and more importantly, raise money for ALS research and services that will help pALS and cALS. It will also allow many pALS and cALS to enjoyable a day out watching their favorite team play ball. So good will come from calling ALS Lou Gehrig's Disease.

Speaking of raising money, my fellow pALS, Jeff Doren, will do his best to raise some bucks for an ALS non-profit again this year. For the third year in a row, Jeff will ride his E-bike to raise funds for the ALS Association's Evergreen Chapter. The Evergreen Chapter, to which both Jeff and I belong, even though Jeff lives in Washington State and I live in Alaska, is headquartered in Kent, Washington.

Jeff, being a baseball fan, will ride in conjunction with Lou Gehrig's Day. Fortunately Jeff has a slow-progressing form of ALS that primarily affects just his legs. This allows him to continue riding his bike to raise crucial money to keep our chapter up and running. In 2019, Jeff raised $11,000.00. Then, with virtual partners riding along in 2020 during the height of the pandemic, he raised over $6,000.00. This year he has set a modest goal of $4,000.00, but, he'll probably blow that goal right out of the water.

When I found out that Jeff would be riding, I asked if Connie and I could sponsor his ride near the town of Index, WA, a small, picturesque located on US-2, better known as Stevens Pass. Since social media plays such a crucial role during Jeff's ride and sponsorships, I wrote the following for him to post on Facebook.

> *I was excited when Jeff announced he'd be riding again this year to raise awareness and money for the Evergreen Chapter of the ALS Association. I'm glad my wife and I can once again sponsor one small part of his multi-week ride.*
>
> *I asked Jeff if we could sponsor him riding in or around the town of Index because of nostalgia. That area has a special place in my heart. Please let me explain.*
>
> *A few days before the end of the year in 1972, my girlfriend and soon to be my wife, Connie, and I jumped in our Jeep with the plan of driving from Denver to Seattle. Since at that time, Seattle was the USA mountaineering and rock climbing mecca, I had wanted to move to there*

for a couple of years. And somehow, I convinced Connie to come along. A couple of days into our drive just east of Moses Lake, our the Jeep threw a rod right through the side of the engine. After having the Jeep towed to a gas station, we caught a bus to Seattle, arriving downtown in the waning hours of 1973. We checked into a fleabag hotel, with only a handful of dollars to our names, and started Seattle adventure.

Within a week of arriving in Seattle, I was extra lucky to get a dream job as an apprentice machinist for what I think was the best machine shop in Seattle. Even better, that job allowed us to upgrade from the skid-row hotel to a modest apartment in Seattle's south end. A couple of days after moving into a second-floor apartment, I happened to look through the apartment window right below ours, and to my surprise, lying on the floor was a bunch of climbing gear. So, I knocked on the door and met Mike, a guy my age, who not only was a climber but, an apprentice machinist. We hit it off right away, and soon we were heading out each weekend to climb in the Cascades. And one place we frequently found ourselves climbing was on the Index Town Wall. Then during the summer of 1974, three other guys and I made one of the first assents of the Mt. Index traverse, climbing the North Peak to the Middle Peak, and finally the Main Peak before descending.

I also have many fond memories of a small café in Index's downtown area. We'd often stop in there after climbing. They had the best milkshakes ever. When we'd drive over Snoqualmie Pass to climb on the east side of the Cascades, we'd be sure to stop in Index on the way home for a meal or a milkshake.

Thanks, Jeff, for riding to raise funds for the Evergreen Chapter. And thank you for letting Connie and me sponsor your ride around the town of Index. I hope when you ride, you'll get a good view of Mt. Index. I think it's one of the prettiest peaks in the Cascades.

Mt. Index, Washington State.

Thinking about Index brought back many good memories, so I both reminisced and refreshed them by Googling some of my past climbs in the area. Imagine my surprise when I ran into a summit registry photo my three climbing partners and I left on the summit in 1974. In July of 2010, thirty-six years after Dave, Steve, and Greg climbed the full Mt. Index Traverse, two climbers happened upon the note we left on the Middle Peak.

July 28, 1974. I have erased the last names of my climbing partners to protect their privacy. After 36 years, the note is a bit hard to read. It says, "July 28, 1974, we got the second leg of the Traverse. Good weather. Great views. Neat climbing. This makes about the 9th or 10th team to try the Traverse. Dave, Steve, Marcel, Greg." I think we used the word "try" because we knew we still had possibly the most challenging climbing ahead of us, climbing from the saddle between the Middle Peak and the Main Peak.

Besides chronic pain from ALS waking me up every night, I have a relativity new malady, possibly anhidrosis,* the body's inability to sweat properly. It's caused by peripheral neuropathy, and makes me to wake up overheated, feeling ten-thousand pins and needles poking my skin from the inside. That feeling is not particularly painful, but it is sure darn annoying and incredibly weird. I go from freezing cold to over-hot; my body is not doing a particularly good job of self-regulating. I try to sleep a little on the cool side, but after waking up shivering, turn on the electric blanket at the lowest temperature, and set the timer for half an hour. Then if I'm lucky, I fall asleep at just the right body temperature. But more times than not, I wake up too cold or too hot. That means while I try to ignore the pain and adjust blankets to moderate my body temperature, I have plenty of time to, figuratively speaking, walk down Memory Lane, recalling past adventures, including mountaineering in the Cascades.

Finding that photo of the old summit registry took me right back to July 1974. Steve and I talked about climbing the Traverse from nearly the first time Mike, the climber from our apartment building, introduced us. Like most folks I climbed with, Steve was a member of the University Climbing Club, and being poor students, they would frequently join Connie and me for the Wednesday night all-you-can-eat pizza night at a pizza place in Burien, near the Seattle Airport. I'm sure when the owner of the pizza joint saw us climbers, he questioned his decision to offer ALL You Can Eat.

Most Wednesday evenings, a half-dozen climbers would converge there. We'd pull a couple of tables together, order a couple of pitchers of root beer, and commence to stuff our faces with endless pieces of all varieties of pizza. While hounding the waitress for even more pizza, we'd talk about climbs we had done and climbs we planned. The Wednesday before we climbed the Index Traverse, we determined the weather would be perfect for the upcoming climb. Steve and Mike couldn't get the weekend free to go climbing, so Greg and I solidified our plans for it. Greg would pick me up Friday evening, and then we'd drive to the Lake Serene trailhead, right below the North Peak.

Not much over an hour from Seattle, we hiked up the incredibly steep trail that parallels the stunning Bridal Veil Falls' left side. Soon we found ourselves on Lake Serene's shoreside, and after a quick dinner, we crawled into our tent for an early night's sleep. No sooner had I zipped my sleeping bag when I heard familiar voices. There was Steve, along with Dave, a tall skinny climber I'd climbed with a couple of times. Steve could come after all. I was glad to see them because of how fun it was to climb with Steve. I also knew both guys were better climbers than I was.

April 21, 2021. Jeff, standing behind his electric bike, and since he is riding in honor of Lou Gehrig, Jeff is dressed to play ball. Behind Jeff are the three peaks of Mt. Index on the left and Mt. Persis on the right. Our climb of the Traverse followed the skyline from the North Peak in the center of the photo, over to the Middle Peak, and then onto the Main Peak. Elevations of the three peaks from left to right, 5991', 5493', and 5360'. Photo courtesy of Jeff's wife, Erin Doran.

The following day after breakfast, we stood at the base of the North Peak and looked at the 4000-foot cliff we'd soon be climbing. We decided that we'd climb together but as two separate teams. Steve and Dave would make one team, and Greg and I the other. We agreed that when the opportunity allowed, we'd switch leads, and if needed, we'd tie the two teams together. Knowing that Steve was the best lead climber of the four of us made me happy, and soon he took off leading up the rock. We further agreed that we'd all four climb simultaneously when possible, which would speed up the climb. And whoever was leading, would, at his discretion, leave protection in the rock for the last person to retrieve. In those days, protection mainly consisted of pitons driven into cracks in the rock, webbing slings that would be wrapped around trees or rocks, and chocks that would be jammed into cracks. Cams, the preferred protection nowadays, wouldn't come along for a few more years. I led as we neared the knife-sharp summit ridge of the North Peak. The climbing was easy enough. We'd climb simultaneously, placing the odd piece of protection here and there. As I made my way up the very airy ridge, Greg was on my rope. We decided if I fell, he'd jump off the opposite side of the ridge. That way, our bodies would be hanging off either side of the ridge and neither of us would fall thousands of feet to our deaths.

By noon, we'd reached the North Peak summit and then rappelled and down-climbed into the North and Middle Peak gap. Obviously, we spent enough time on the Middle Peak summit to leave a note in the summit registry, though I have zero recollection of doing so. The sloppy writing on the registry note looks like mine, but I seldom signed, let alone wrote anything in summit registers. Even back then, I tried to do my best to "Leave no Trace," so signing a registry was somewhat of an act against my moral compass. Perhaps that's why I don't remember the note we left? We down-climbed and rappelled into the saddle between the Middle and Main Peak where we ate dinner and settled into our bivouac for the night. Good anchors and slings secured us in our sleeping bags so that we wouldn't roll off the nearly vertical 3000-foot cliff in the middle of the night.

After a quick breakfast the next morning, we started up the last leg of the climb, and by midmorning we were on top of the Main Peak. An easy scramble along the long ridgeline followed by an easy hike found us back at Lake Serene. After collecting our tents, we drove home, knowing we had accomplished something few people had. All these years later I'm particularly proud of that climb, and when ALS robs me of sleep, I take comfort in dreaming of it and many other climbs.

If I'm lucky nowadays, when pain or an uncomfortable body temperature wakes me, I quickly fall asleep again and dream of better days. When lying awake, I recall other climbs, some with the guys I climbed the three Mt. Index Peaks with. Possibly two weekends after the Index climb, Dave, Steve, and I climbed the North Ridge of the 9415-foot, Mt. Stuart. I didn't know when I left Connie and our one-year-old son Zach early that Saturday morning, that the Stuart climb would set in motion a significant change in our lives.

We arrived at the Ingalls Lake trailhead about lunchtime and started the 4.5-mile hike to the lake with our packs and ropes on our backs. The hike was stunningly beautiful, even though excruciating cramps in both calf muscles made the hike almost impossible. For the first time in my life, I couldn't keep up with my hiking and climbing partners. It's not like I wasn't in shape. Most days I walked three miles to work and back. And most evenings after work, I jumped into the pool at the apartment we were renting and swam laps. Not to mention, my job kept me on my feet all day, only sitting down for lunch. Steve came to the rescue. He had some salt tablets in his first-aid kit, and suggested I take a couple with lots of water. The pills, water and sitting for about 20-minutes caused a miraculous recovery. I nearly ran the rest of the way to our camp below the 20 pitch North Ridge.

Unlike the climb on Index, where the weather was perfect, light rain, a strong north wind, and occasional snowflake graced our start up the North Ridge of Mt. Stuart. We talked about calling off the climb, but went for it, knowing we could always rappel off the climb if the weather didn't improve. Except for the wind, it did.

The climb was in the shade with a strong wind blowing on us, so we all got miserably cold. When we were belaying the lead climber or sitting waiting for our turn to climb, we shivered and looked forward to our turn to move again so we could warm up. I was extremely happy when it came to my turn to climb the second-to-the-last pitch before the summit ridge. Being cold from sitting, I took off up that pitch knowing I'd warm up, and that soon we'd be on the summit. Further, once we hit the summit, we'd be heading down the Cascadian Couloir on the other side of the mountain out of the wind. Perhaps that's why I climbed that pitch extra fast, placing almost no protection on the 5.8 lead. When I belayed Steve up to the belay ledge after that pitch, he said something along with these lines, "Nice climbing, but damn, you should have placed a lot more protection." Rightly so. He went on to cuss me out, reminding me that every climber in a team is only as safe as the unsafest climber. Had I fallen with so little protection, it could have put the safety of all of us at risk.

Starting down the other side, we warmed up as I suspected we would. But out of the wind and into the sun, it was almost too hot. Soon all three of us had stripped down to single layers. We had also miscalculated how much time it would require to climb the route. We knew the North Ridge was a serious climb, but it had taken much longer than we hoped. Not wanting to get caught in the dark during our descent, we literally ran down the mountain. But to no avail. We soon found ourselves in ever-fading light, and none of us had as much as a small flashlight, let alone headlamps. Then to add insult to injury, even that late in the summer we ran into deep snow. The snow had long ago consolidated into hard-packed snow, so hiking down was easy. However, dangerously hidden in it were massive tree wells, meaning the snowfield was full of hundreds of hidden crevasses. By the time we made our way through these, it was completely dark. We all fell into tree wells. If we were lucky, we'd fall only a few feet until we'd stop on a branch of the evergreen tree. Sometimes we'd fall twenty or more feet, stopping only when we hit the ground. Fortunately, the tree branches slowed our falls, and no one got hurt. But I can tell you from firsthand experience; it's not easy to climb out of a tree well. One tree well I fell into was especially deep, Steve had to carefully lower me a rope, and he and Dave had to haul me up out of it.

It was way after midnight when we tiredly stumbled down the last few yards to our car. I don't remember if Steve and Dave had to be at work that Monday morning, but I did. As they drove back over Blewett and Snoqualmie Passes, I slept soundly in the back seat dreaming of our successful climb.

I had already learned, at the time when you're freezing, miserable, clinging to a vertical rock for dear life, and wondering why the hell you'd be so stupid to exposure yourself to the dangers of climbing, you say to yourself, "I'll never do that again. I'm done climbing." But when safely back on the ground, warm and dry, you can't wait to do it again. Nothing is more rewarding than getting way out of one's comfort zone and surviving the challenge. When back in the real "sane" world, you know you accomplished something to be proud of. And that was always more rewarding and fulfilling to me than money.

It was about 4:00 a.m. when my two climbing partners dropped me off at our apartment. Before we left, I had told Connie I should be home around 5:00 p.m. on Sunday, 8:00 tops. I was way late getting home, and knew Connie would be extra worried. If I could have called, I would have, but we didn't have a phone in our apartment. Even knowing she would be worried, what I saw when I walked in the door shook me to my core. I had expected to find her curled up snugly in bed. Instead, she was sitting in an armchair holding our baby Zach, crying. She told me she thought I might be dead. Through her sobs, she went on, "I had no idea who to call first." She said she planned to start by calling what she assumed was the closest sheriff's department when it got light enough to walk the five or six blocks to the nearest payphone. Seeing the woman I loved crying made me feel like a real jerk, and I vowed I'd do what I could to find some other adventurous activity I could do with my family. Being somewhat addicted to climbing, giving it up would be like a junkie giving up his heroin, but my family and their happiness was more important than my desire to risk my life climbing.

I can't remember when Steve first said something like this to me, "I suggest you stop climbing. You take too many risks, and you seem to have bad luck. I don't want to see another friend die." But the next time he saw Connie after our Stuart climb, he told her the same thing.

Steve's words and the memory Connie in tears weighed on me as Greg and I headed off a couple of weeks later to climb Mt. Slesse, right across the border in British Columbia. The solution of what adventure we could do as a family came to me on the summit of Mt. Slesse. As Greg and I stood on the summit of that majestic mountain, I looked nearly a hundred miles to the west and past the city of Vancouver to the ocean. Maybe it was the thin air affecting my brain, but in a daydream, I could see Connie, Zach, and me on a sailboat sailing over the horizon seeking new adventures and new lands.

Jump forward a dozen years to the banks of the Fraser River in the town of Surrey, BC, a suburb of Vancouver. There we launched our newly built schooner, *Terra Nova*, and I again thought of that gloriously sunny day when Greg and I stood on the summit of Mt. Slesse. We were now living that daydream from all those years ago, fulfilling the prophecy of seeking adventures while exploring new lands. Translated from Latin, terra nova, means new land or unexplored land.

Though ALS now has me confined to a wheelchair with no hope of ever climbing or sailing again, I take great comfort in remembering all the adventures I had in the mountains and on and in the water. There is no doubt in my mind that those adventures, and especially the ones I shared with my family, help me deal with this horrendous disease. I was wired to need adventure in my life, and fortunately, Connie was, too.

As I lie in bed, trying to sleep, I also think about the people I've been privileged to share the other end of a rope with, hoist a sail with, or have so many different adventures with. I was lucky to meet those folks, let alone do extra fun things with them. Let me tell you a bit more about my adventuring friends.

First JEFF. One good thing about having ALS is that I've met many great people I wouldn't have otherwise. Jeff, like me, enjoys woodworking. Almost in reach as I write this, I can see two different pieces of Jeff's craftsmanship [see below]. And like me, Jeff likes being outdoors in the mountains. This desire to be outside is possibly why Jeff was a volunteer search and rescue guy for many years. A couple of years ago, Jeff sent me his book titled, <u>Search on Mount St. Helens</u>. In it he chronicles his experiences with his German Shepard dog, Ben, searching for victims of the May 1980 blast of volcanic ash, mud, and other debris. Though out of print, I found it on a few used book sites online. It's also probably available through inter-library loans. If you're interested in search and rescue or the impact of the Mount Saint Helens eruption, this book is worth reading.

2021. The wine bottle holder designed to keep the cork from drying out seems to defy gravity, and a wooden Fibonacci gauge, were both gifts made by Jeff.

Now in order of the signatures, we left on the Index North Peak register.

DAVE: I lost track of Dave, but I know he became an engineer and was working in Seattle. A Google search didn't result in anything conclusive.

STEVE: Steve became a famous climber, climbing all over the world, including here in Alaska. After the Mt. Stuart climb, he and I did a few less serious rock climbs, mostly near Leavenworth, Washington, and some "buildering" in Seattle. Yes, I said, buildering and not bouldering. While I belayed him from one building, Steve climbed the wall on the Saint Cabrini Hospital in Seattle when the cops and one truly angry nun showed up. The nun, in her

1974. Lunchtime for Steve.

very German accent, kept yelling, "This not Mount Rainer." And since Connie, holding Zach in her arms, was watching us climb, the nun had a few not-so-very-kind words about mothering for Connie, too. After the nun concluded giving us the what-for, the cop told us, "You have to take old nuns with a grain of salt." He then directed us to climb the drainpipes under the Freeway Bridge of the Ship Canal, already one of our favorite places to climb.

In the late 1990s, a sailing friend invited Connie and me to a climbing slideshow in Port Townsend. To our surprise, we found out the guest speaker would be Steve. We had arrived early enough that Connie and I had some time to chat with him. I think it was at that meeting when Steve invited me to meet him at the Vertical World Climbing Gym in Seattle. When we met there, Steve climbed the most challenging routes while I belayed him. When my turn came, I stuck to the easy climbs, but we still had fun.

GREG: I was negligent when it came to keeping up with Greg. Unless we maybe met in the late 70s at Mike's funeral, the last time we met, or possibly even talked, was our climb on Mt. Slesse. It's not like we didn't have a great climb or didn't get along. We did. And if ever there was an amiable climbing partner, it would have been Greg. Usually, when friends don't contact each other, it's a two-way street, but in this case, I didn't have a phone, and Greg did. So, when I stumbled onto the photo of the1974 summit registry I felt I had to Google Greg. The search resulted in an address; I wrote him via US Post and was happy when he emailed me back. We are now exchanging emails and catching up on the last 47 years.

MIKE: I've often thought about Mike. I mentioned that Greg might have been at Mike's funeral because, other than Mike's sister, Linda, I think everyone else there was a climber or a climber's female partner.

Now that I'm staring death in the face, as everyone who is told they have a terminal disease does, I recall how lucky I was when while climbing with Mike on Mt. Rainier in the winter of 1974. Un-roped, I fell straight down sixty feet

1974. Greg down climbing along the ridge of the Index Traverse.

before I wedged tight into a very deep crevasse on Mt. Rainier. I should have died that day. I indeed owe my life to Mike, as he would owe his life to me later that day. It's just short of a miracle that our bodies aren't still lying under the Nisqually Glacier on Mt. Rainier. So, I feel in part, that I owe the subsequent years of a happy life to Mike. That is why I wonder whether I could have done more to prevent Mike from committing suicide.

Ever since we met Mike, he was either overwhelmingly happy or in the deepest depression I'd ever seen. And sadly the depression became more and more prevalent; totally debilitating. A year or so before he took his own life, at the very depth of his depression, he got help from the State of Washington Mental Health Services. A year later, budget cuts hit the Mental Health Services, and he lost the help he desperately needed. Seeing no hope, he jumped nearly 200 feet to the water of Ship Canal below the Aurora Bridge in Seattle.

Mike is not the only person I've known who has taken his own life, but because of the bond we made surviving Mt. Rainier, his death affected me deeply. And because I know firsthand how devastating suicide can be to the survivors, as bad as ALS might get for me, I can't see blowing my brains out, overdosing on drugs, or drowning myself. I couldn't do that to the people I care about. I support medical aid in dying, and I won't rule that out for myself. But the right to choose death over living with a cruel disease is a far cry from suicide.

I have strayed far from Lou Gehrig and baseball. However, when Jeff said he'd ride in and around the town of Index, that was the spark that ignited the fire in my memory banks. Many good and not-so-good memories have helped me pass time and ignore the pain and discomfort brought on by ALS. Now Jeff, I, and the thousands of others hope to be mega-successful raising money for ALS on Lou Gehrig's Day. That desperately needed money will help, not only for the local chapters of the ALS Association, but the research that, with any luck, will find a cure for this God-awful disease. Meanwhile, I'll do my best to live each day to the fullest. And that includes many more walks down Memory Lane.

**Anhidrosis is the inability to sweat properly. I try not to play Dr. Google, but when I Googled Anhidrosis, I found a way-too-technical-for-me study of anhidrosis in ALS patients. It reported that as ALS progress, 40% of the people studied developed or partially developed anhidrosis in parts of their bodies. This may be why I so easily overheat.*

Happy Days

10 May 2021

Forty-eight years ago today, Thursday afternoon, May 10, 1973, I took off work an hour early and walked a couple of blocks to the bus stop. As I nervously waited for the bus, I thought about what lay ahead and hoped the bus would be on time. After a couple of minutes of waiting, I saw the bus was indeed running on time. Even better, as the bus approached the stop, I saw a very cute girl staring out the window at me. As I climbed the stairs into the bus, I reached into my pocket and pulled out two dimes. Then after dropping the dimes into the toll box, I headed down the aisle as I heard the clang, clang of the dimes working their way down the chute into the change box. Soon, I was sitting down next to the cute girl I had seen from outside the bus. I noticed she was wearing a homemade maternity blouse, and as I reached for her hand, she reached back. I give her a kiss, and we chatted as the bus made its way towards downtown Seattle.

About 15 minutes later, the bus stopped; we got off and, holding hands walked up the hill towards the King County Courthouse. In the lobby, we quickly read the directory, and finding the judge's name we were looking for we boarded the elevator. Upon reaching the proper floor, we quickly found the Court Clerk's office, and paid her $20.00; she gave some paperwork and then directed us into the courtroom. A few minutes later, in walked the judge, his secretary, and the clerk we had already met. After some quick introductions, the judge said, "Do you, Connie, take this man to be your lawfully wedded husband, for better or worse, to death do you part?" And fortunately, Connie answered, "I do." The judge then asked me, "Do you, Marcel, take this woman to be your lawfully wedded wife, for better or worse, to death do you part?" I, possibly with knees shaking, said, "I do." The judge then said, "Under the power vested in me by the State of Washington, I now pronounce you husband and wife." I no longer remember if he said, "You can now kiss the bride," but I'm sure I did. Less than half an hour earlier, we had walked into the courthouse, single but totally committed to each other. Now, in the eyes of the law, we walked out of the courthouse legally married.

All these years later, I remember most of the details of the rest of that evening. We walked a dozen blocks to the Seattle Monorail and then took it to the Seattle Center, about a five-minute ride. Seattle Center, just like the Monorail, are leftovers from the 1962 Seattle's World Fair. Once there, we walked straight into the old Armory building and headed for the Food Circus, yet another relic of the World's Fair. Unlike today, the Food Circus, with a new name in 2021, had no chain restaurants, but had a wide variety of food choices. We probably chose from the Mexican or the Italian fast-food counters. After we ate, we took the clear plastic Bubbleator, now long gone, up to the mezzanine that overlooked the food court. At the time, the mezzanine was loaded with import stores, a photo gallery, and at least one art gallery. Even for me, a guy who HATES shopping, it was a fun place to window shop. It was probably there, where I first saw Russian matryoshka nesting dolls, a cooking wok, or a whole host of things a guy growing up in rural Colorado would have never seen before. After making the complete 360-degree circuit, we undoubtedly rode the Bubbleator down to the basement stores. A used bookstore, located in the far corner from the Bubbleator and stairs, I think was a branch of Shorey's Used and Rare Books, the famous Seattle's Pioneer Square used bookstore. Both stores were total chaos and a book hoarder's dream come true. But with tons of used books, used magazines, and even stacks upon stacks of old newspapers stacked floor to ceiling, they must have been the Seattle Fire Marshal's worst nightmare. As much as Connie and I could have spent hours digging through the old books, the musty smell of old books and the mildew that seemed to ooze out of every nook, cranny and even caked the concrete ceiling drove us to seek fresh air in a few minutes.

Before leaving, we went back to the Food Circus to an ice cream shop full of incredibly delicious flavors and where we first saw waffle cones. Their cones were gigantic. After you ordered, you'd watch it come off the press, and seconds later it was filled with a good pint of ice cream.

Ice cream in hand we walked to the Flag Pavilion, where all the fifty states' flags were displayed. Our game was to see if we could figure out which flag belonged to which state. Many we recognized right away, but about a third of them kept us guessing. Then off we went down the hill to the International fountain, which is still my favorite fountain in the world. The fountain sits in a 220-foot diameter basin with 137 mist nozzles, 77 fleur-de-lis nozzles, 57 micro-shooting nozzles, and four super-high shooting nozzles that blast water 120 feet into the sky. More impressive than those stats, the various nozzles are perfectly timed to shoot water with ever-changing music. With water shutting off and on and at varying pressures, one can sit by the fountain watching the water and music show for hours. Even more fun than watching the water is watching the kids playing in and around the fountain. I'm sure that spring day forty-eight years ago was too chilly for kids to be playing in the fountain, but kids were indeed running in and around the fountain's basin.

After sitting by the fountain, enjoying watching kids and the water show while eating our ice cream, we walked a couple of blocks through the park to the Seattle Opera House. Our wedding day treat to ourselves was going to watch Marcel Marceau perform his magnificent pantomime act. Even sitting in one of the last rows in the nose-bleed section of the auditorium, we couldn't have found better entertainment to celebrate our wedding day.

After the show, we took the Monorail back downtown, and caught the bus home. Arriving at our apartment around midnight and climbing the stairs to the second floor, I opened the door to our apartment. I abided by tradition and carried my new bride over the threshold. Even back then being up that late was not my cup of tea, so we were soon crashed out in bed. I had to get up early on Friday morning for work. There would be no honeymoon then, or ever. But, I was bursting with happiness to be married to the gal I loved. A honeymoon would have been nice but it was far from necessary. Beginning a life with Connie was all I needed to brim from ear to ear with overwhelming happiness.

A bit over two months after our wedding day, our son, Zachariah, Zach for short, was born. I was thrilled to be a father, and I loved not only our new baby, but I loved his mother, the cute girl I first saw through the bus window.

As we celebrate our 48th anniversary and 49 years together, I wonder if the beautiful woman I love would have said, "Yes" if she could have seen the future. Knowing our golden years would be spent with me having ALS, I wouldn't have faulted her if she had said, "No." I hate putting the burden of caregiving on my bride. Even if we had a crystal ball back then and could have seen the twists and turns our married life would take, I would have answered the judge with a million "Yes's." I still love that woman, and I cherish all the Happy Days we have accumulated in our 49 years together

 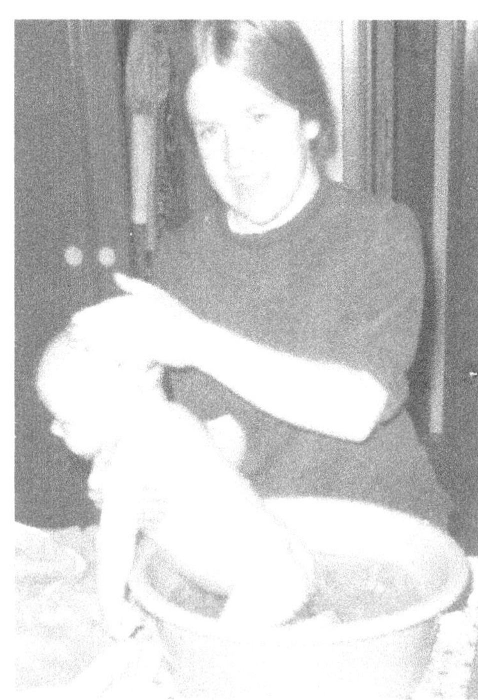

1973. Connie shortly after Zach was born.

May 2021. Connie and her baby, Bella, a week before our anniversary.

Opera, Dreams, and Death

8 August 2021

A few nights ago, as I was getting ready for bed, I was listening to the audio-book *Death is but a Dream* by hospice and palliative care doctor Christopher Kerr and English professor Carine M. Mardorossian. As my wife, Connie, lowered me onto my hospital bed from our rolling standing lift, she asked, "Did someone recommend that book, or did you stumble upon it?" After she set me on the edge of the bed, and before she lifted my legs onto the bed, since I can't talk, I typed into my phone, "Aria Code." I think she was a bit surprised, but after just a couple of seconds, she said, "That makes sense; someone is always dying in most operas. Either they die of consumption, or some bad guy kills a good guy." As I nodded agreement, I typed, "*Tosca*, by Puccini." Since we once saw this opera at a live performance, she understood.

ALS has given me a neurogenic bladder, which means the muscles that would normally push urine out of my body have significantly weakened, causing urine to just dribble out. That means I spend a lot of time sitting on the toilet, which also means I have a lot of time to listen to podcasts. And one of my favorites in my eclectic mix of podcasts is Aria Code, a podcast produced by the New York Metropolitan Opera and WQXR Radio and hosted by Rhiannon Giddens. In the podcast, Ms. Giddens and her guests digest the meaning of a single aria from a different opera each time. To understand an individual aria, they must explain the opera's central theme. To do this, Ms. Gidden's guests often compare a modern story with the opera's plot. Since I'm a big fan of anything composed by Puccini, I was recently re-listening to the Aria Code episode about one of my favorite operas, *Tosca.*

In that edition, one guest was Dr. Christopher Kerr, who said when people near the end of life, they often have very vivid dreams about people they have loved in their lifetimes. Or, they become fixated on the memory of a beloved spouse or someone they have loved. One tear-jerking story he recounted was about an elderly widower who deeply missed his recently deceased wife. He would visit her grave every day, spending hours sitting or kneeling by the tombstone. One day when his daughter came to pick him up from the graveyard, she found him walking in the snow. First confused, she then saw he was making the shape of a heart around his wife's grave. As she escorted him to the car, she could see he was sick. When he didn't get better, she took him to the hospital, where it was confirmed that he had suffered a massive heart attack while making a heart in the snow. After entering hospice, because he wasn't going to get better, Dr. Kerr said, the elderly gentleman literally died of a broken heart.

Connie was right about a villain killing a good guy. In *Tosca,* the villain is Baron Scarpia, the chief of police and the good guy is Mario Cavaradossi, an artist and political activist. And a beautiful woman; Floria Tosca, an opera singer. Cavaradossi is in love with Tosca, and being a jealous villain, Scarpia has Cavaradossi arrested and tortured for his political activism. Cavaradossi is sentenced to death, and in his final hour of life, knowing he is about to die,

Cavaradossi enters a daydream about a passionate night he spent with Tosca. In the third and last act of the opera, Cavaradossi sings about the daydream, in the aria, *e Lucevan le Stelle*, translation, "And the Stars were Shining." Because of Puccini's genius, the instruments that accompany the lyrics make this aria make it one of the most moving tenor arias in the world of opera.

Back to *Death is but a Dream* and the end of life. Just as Cavaradossi knows he is close to death when he sings, *e Lucevan le Stelle*.

My life is nearing the end, but is not imminent; it could be months away. I'm defying the odds living nearly eight years with bulbar ALS, which has a life expectancy of slightly over two years.

As many people do when they near the end of life, I have been enjoying very vivid dreams about people and places from my past. These dreams include people I haven't thought about for decades. There was even one dream where I was in my mother's side bedroom talking to my grandmother, where she lay close to death. Just like she did when I was four years old, she said in the dream, "Come in, I have a lemon drop candy for you." The dream was so real, I could smell the candy she always kept by her bedside for my siblings and me.

Whereas most dreams near the end of life tend to be positive dreams full of love and loved ones, according to Dr. Kerr's research a handful of dreams can be frightening and traumatic. Wartime veterans might have realistic dreams that take them back into the horrors of war. Or a criminal might have nightmares about their illegal misdeeds, and feel guilty about them. I'm no exception to when it comes to nightmares. Most of my dreams are not bad, but in one recent dream, I saw myself as a fully-grown adult sitting on the floor with my back against a cinderblock wall. On my lap was a young girl of about five years of age, crying; she was frightened of something or someone. As I hugged her, doing my best to give her comfort, in walked my stepmother, Mary, saying, "Give her to me." When I exclaimed, "NO," Mary yelled, "I said give her to me!" I then yelled, "Fuck you. You can go to hell." With that, Mary grabbed my head and started slamming it against the wall. The little girl ran and cowered in the corner of the room. I then stood up, towering over my abusive step-mother; grabbing her by the shoulders, I slammed her head hard against the wall. Mary slid down the wall screaming in pain. I then said, "I could easily kill your right now, but I want you to live a long miserable life full of self-inflicted pain." As I said those words, I looked over my shoulder. There stood my father with his hands in his pockets, calmly looking on, just like he had done a thousand times in real life as Mary beat my two sisters and me. In the dream, I grabbed the little girl's hand and walked out the door. That is when I woke up.

Unlike I had hundreds of times before, with cold sweat coving my body and adrenaline flowing through every vein in my body, this time I woke up ecstatic with a feeling of euphoria. Now awake, I wondered who the girl was. Was she my older sister, Andree, or my younger sister, Chelly, or could she have been one of my three stepsisters? Surely it was one of them. Am I finally coming to terms with the violence and trauma I suffered as a child? One thing I'm extremely proud of: my sister's, Andree, and Chelly, and I broke the chain of abuse and became loving parents to our children.

Many of my sleeping hours are now full of dreams about my beautiful wife, our son, Zach, his wife, Jenn, and our three grandsons. I often dream of when Connie and I were first married, possibly the happiest days of my life. I see us as the happy young couple we were. Sometimes, we are walking hand in hand, pushing our happy and inquisitive toddler sitting in his baby stroller. Or walking down a sidewalk with a young Zach between us, holding up both of his arms and holding our hands. Every time we come to a curb, we lift our son by his arms and swing him up or down from the curb as he squeals and laughs with joy. Sometimes, I see one of our grandsons substituting for Zach as the young boy in my dreams. These dreams bring me great joy, and when I wake from one of them, I'm very happy.

I also frequently dream of the men I have been fortunate to work with over the years, including my older brother, Fred. I say men because I have primarily worked in male-dominated fields. In one recurring dream, I see myself over 45-years ago standing behind a metal lathe, and across the room from me, standing behind a milling machine, is my workmate, Roger. Over the noise made by our respective machine tools, we chat about beagles, other dogs, farm animals, and other subjects. Hanging on the wall to my right, about halfway between Roger and me, is a radio tuned to Seattle's premier classical music station, KING FM. Coming from that radio is one of many operas we listen to most afternoons. That dream shows that I owe much of my life-long love of opera and beagles to Roger and our many, many hours together.

As I write this, Connie's birthday is just a day away. In our fifty years together, we have seldom given material gifts to each other, finding it better to spend our money on essentials. This year, I hope to give her a couple more years of life together. ALS prevents me from giving much to our relationship in return for all she does for me. I rely on her more and more, and with each passing week, I become more of a burden on the woman I love. Despite that, I think she wants me around a bit longer. We both know that ALS is a cruel disease, and that a common cold or prolonged power outage could quickly end my life. So who knows when my time will come? I do know that I can die in peace, knowing the beautiful girl I fell in love with as teens and stayed true to all these years will be by my side when I leave this earth. I hope to die listening to a beautiful aria holding my loving wife's hand. Music and my wife's presence will ensure I die peacefully.

Closing

30 May 2021

Early in 2016, when I posted a couple of my health updates on Facebook, my first intent was to inform my family and friends how I was doing without writing dozens of emails. Secondly, I wanted to leave a little of me for my grandsons and their kids. But a doctor friend read the Facebook postings, and thought my words would help others dealing with ALS and other diseases. Upon his and others' encouragement, I decided to compile my essays into a book. Knowing nothing about compiling a book, Blanche, a friend from when we both worked at Sheldon Jackson College, introduced me to the extraordinarily gifted Dana Anderson. With that introduction and a lot of work by Dana, my first book, *Just Another Adventure*, was born. Since my ALS has been progressing slowly, I continued to write, and I set my goal to write a trilogy of books about my life living with ALS. About a year and a half later, my second book, *The Adventure Continues* hit the online bookseller's shelves. Now, with this book, *The Last Adventure*, I have reached my goal, which, of course, makes me happy. And if I keep defying the odds, who knows, maybe I'll write a fourth book. If I do, I guess I'll have to title it, *I Guess I Was Wrong.* And that, too, would make me happy.

Since all the proceeds from all of my book sales are donated to ALS nonprofits, please consider buying or encouraging a friend to buy one of my other books. Thank you.

Construction Tips Appendix

Theory

Based on Maslow's Hierarchy of Needs and guided by Revised Amyotrophic Lateral Sclerosis Functional Rating Scale (ALSFRS-R)

I may have heard of Maslow's Hierarchy of Needs in some time far distant past but would have scratched my head and shrugged my shoulders if you asked me to explain it. So, when Dana Anderson suggested it might be helpful to launch ideas for coping with ALS' specific issues using my experience with construction and ALS, I adapted Maslow's Hierarchy of Needs to build Marcel's Hierarchy of ALS Needs. I have always loved achieving one's goals by going down parallel paths simultaneously, so I went to Wikipedia to learn about Maslow's. And since I had self-evaluated my ALS using the Revised Amyotrophic Lateral Sclerosis Functional Rating Scale (ALSFRS-R) in February 2021, I used those results to throw into the mix.

Maslow's theory is summarized in the pyramid diagram below. His "needs" are shown in black text. Marcel's Hierarchy of ALS Needs are shown in the chart below. Just like a house needs a strong foundation, both Maslow's and Marcel's Needs start at the bottom of the pyramid. Without the "Basic needs" none of the rest can be achieved.

Maslow's Hierarchy of Needs

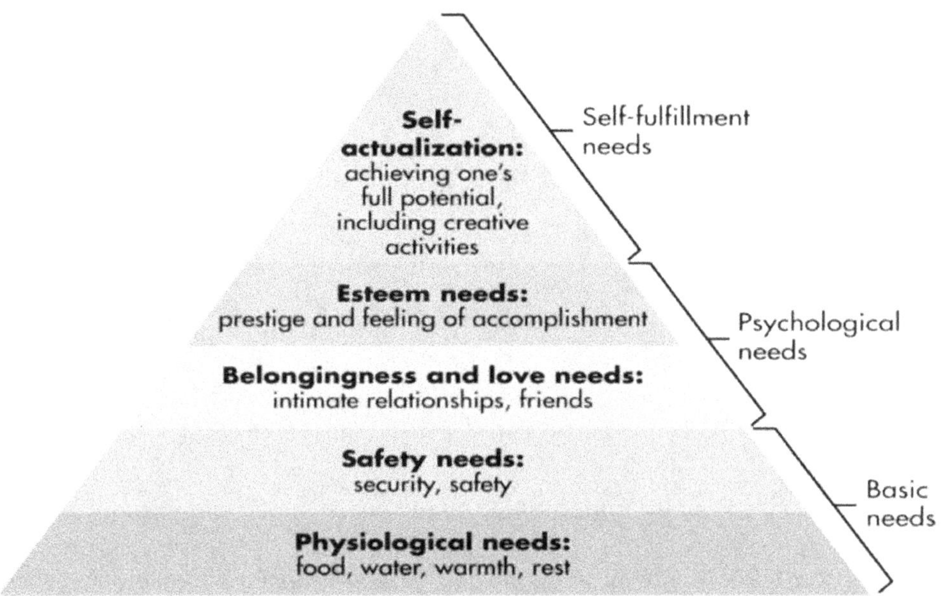

Marcel's Hierarchy of ALS Needs

Self Fulfillment Needs	Happiness
Psychological Needs	Anger and Frustration Control Caregivers, Medical Needs, and Family
Basic Needs	Walkers, Wheelchairs, Grab Bars and Poles Ramps, Doors, Bathrooms and other Handicap Modifications

When living with ALS or any disability, all humans have the same basic physiological needs. However, as disabled people's physiological needs must also include things that non-disabled person can do without. Things like ramps, doors that are wide enough to accommodate our wheelchairs, to name two.

Further, as we go up Maslow's Pyramid, disabled people also need security and safety. In the early stages of ALS or many other disabilities, first a cane and then a walker will help prevent falls. As our legs become weaker, we will depend on a wheelchair.

For our mental well-being, we have the exact psychological needs as able-bodied people; the need to love and be loved. Loving caregivers and compassionate healthcare personnel provide these for us.

We also need self-esteem and the feeling we have accomplished things. Just controlling anger and frustration, and living life as fully as our disabilities will allow should boost our self-esteem.

At the pinnacle, self-actualization by achieving our full potential in life, even when living with a disability should be a worthy goal. Handicap modifications will make reaching the peak of happiness at the top of the pyramid easier to achieve.

Since I'm living with ALS, talking about modifications to one's living quarters to fit that disability is the easiest for me. But these modifications are applicable for many other disabilities. I will also use the Revised Amyotrophic Lateral Sclerosis Functional Rating Scale (ALSFRS-R). It stratifies severity of amyotrophic lateral sclerosis (ALS), including respiratory function and can be used as a tool to project what modifications will be needed and when they will be required.

For pALS [persons with ALS] and cALS [caregivers for ALS] not familiar with the ALSFRS-R, the highest possible score is 48; one that a fully functioning person would achieve. As a person's ALS progresses, points are subtracted. The sum of those points is a marker that doctors and others can use to track one's ALS progression. The score can be used to predict when a person will need modifications and is also used to track how effective a potential new drug is during drug trials. During the 2019 to 2021 trials of the drug AMX0035, the ALSFRS-R was used to show AMX0035 slows progression based on comparing those taking the drug in a double-blind study to those taking a placebo.

In the chart below my ALSFRS-R results from February 2021 are high-lighted in gray.

Task	Score	Description
Speech	4	Normal
	3	Detectable speech disturbance
	2	Intelligible with repeating
	1	Speech combined with non-vocal communications
	0	Loss of useful speech
Salivation	4	Normal
	3	Slight but definite excess of saliva in mouth; may have nighttime drooling
	2	Moderately excessive saliva; may have minimal drooling
	1	Marked excess of saliva with some drooling
	0	Marked drooling; requires constant tissue or handkerchief
Swallowing	4	Normal eating habits
	3	Early eating problems; occasional choking
	2	Dietary consistency changes
	1	Needs supplemental tube feedings
	0	Nothing by mouth; exclusively parenteral or enteral feeding
Handwriting	4	Normal
	3	Slow or sloppy; all words are legible
	2	Not all words are legible
	1	Able to grip pen but unable to write
	0	Unable to grip pen

Task	Score	Description
Cutting food and handling utensils	4	Normal
	3	Somewhat slow and clumsy but no help needed
	2	Can cut most foods although clumsy and slow; some help needed
	1	Food must be cut by someone but can still feed slowly
	0	Needs to be fed
Dressing and Hygiene	4	Normal function
	3	Independent and complete self-care with effort or decreased efficiency
	2	Intermittent assistance or substitute methods
	1	Needs attendant for self-care
	0	Total dependence
Turning in bed and adjusting bed-clothes	4	Normal
	3	Somewhat slow and clumsy but no help needed
	2	Can turn alone or adjust sheets but with great difficulty
	1	Can initiate but not turn or adjust sheets alone
	0	Helpless
Walking	4	Normal
	3	Early ambulation difficulties
	2	Walks with assistance
	1	Non-ambulatory functional movement
	0	No purposeful leg movement
Climbing Stairs	4	Normal
	3	Slow
	2	Mild unsteadiness or fatigue
	1	Needs assistance.
	0	Cannot do

Task	Score	Description
Dyspnea (Labored Breathing)	4	None
	3	Occurs when walking
	2	Occurs with one or more of the following: eating, bathing, dressing
	1	Occurs at rest, difficulty breathing when either sitting or lying
	0	Significant difficulty, considering using mechanical respiratory support
Orthopnea (Discomfort breathing when lying flat)	4	None
	3	Some difficulty sleeping at night due to shortness of breath; does not routinely use >2 pillows
	2	Needs extra pillows in order to sleep (>2)
	1	Can only sleep, sitting up
	0	Unable to sleep
Respiratory insufficiency	4	None
	3	Intermittent use of BiPAP
	2	Continuous use of BiPAP during the night
	1	Continuous use of BiPAP during the night and day
	0	Invasive mechanical ventilation by intubation or tracheostomy
	10	**Total Score of 48 possible**
No		Patients with gastrostomy and >50% daily nutrition intake via G-tube

At first glance, the ALSFRS-R can be a tad confusing. However, if you look back at the category, Walking, if your score is 4, you are walking normally and will not need a ramp to access your home. But if your score is 3, then it is time to build or have a ramp built, knowing by the time your score is 2, you will need a ramp

Practice

My expertise in life is and has been designing, creating, repairing and constructing machinery and buildings. This expertise has served me and my wife well since ALS has entered our lives. Late in 2018, after seeing several posts on the various ALS support sites asking for suggestions on home modifications, I started a group page dedicated to handicap accessibility modifications. Using Maslow and the ALSFRS-R to organize and clarify Marcel's Hierarchy of Needs, this Tips section brings to fore items specific to the basic needs. It also discusses some construction considerations that will ease implementation and perhaps save the cost of having to re-do something because it wasn't done correctly in the first place.

My wife and I built our home specifically to accommodate some of the needs of her recently-widowed 75-year-old mother who was to moving to Sitka, AK to live with us. We made sure the floors had no rugs on which to trip, included an accessible bedroom and bathroom on the main level, and built but two steps with railings to enter the house. We never anticipated needing these accommodations for me, but they have served us well. Not a day goes by when we don't appreciate the ensuite main floor bedroom and easy access to the garage.

Your home may need major as well as minor structural accommodations; doors widened, carpets replaced with a hard surface, and even something as simple as light switches lowered, raised or voice-activated. With proper handicap modifications and the right equipment, and there is no reason why a disabled person can't live a happy and productive life.

The "Construction 101" section, though somewhat theoretical, addresses important considerations before going to the hardware store.

Actual construction specifics begin with building ramps, followed generally by bathroom and bedroom needs.

As I compose this, the power needs at my desk come to mind. I'm typing on my computer, which needs an outlet and another one is needed for the printer. Also on my desk requiring power are a nebulizer, a BIPAP machine, and a blood pressure cuff. Then there are specific "outlets" to charge my phone and other special equipment. Do not short yourselves on power and other "outlets."

Marcel at his desk in Sitka.

Construction 101 -
Function, Aesthetics, and Cost

Nearly 50 years ago in one of my high school shop classes, we learned that the three things we must consider when designing anything are: function, aesthetics, and cost. I've tried to keep those three things in mind when designing across the years, however the balancing act of doing so is not always easy.

Let's say we are designing a new handicap-accessible bathroom, and want a roll-in shower. The least expensive way to build the shower floor and walls might be to brush waterproof urethane on plywood surfaces, but that wouldn't be as aesthetically pleasing as ceramic tile. On the other extreme, we could do the surfaces with imported Italian marble, but that would break the bank. So, we must balance our budget while building something that works well but looks good, too.

The cost of a project might be the trickiest consideration. We need to consider initial costs as well as long-term costs. We might save on the upfront cost if we put a double pane window in our new bathroom, but if we install a triple pane window, the upfront cost may pay for itself in energy savings down the line. We can buy an inexpensive faucet, but will we have to replace it in two years, instead of 30 years? If the low-cost faucet needs replaced in two years, then our original savings was not a bargain.

When we built our house, I cut initial costs by using inexpensive bathroom fans. Though I knew better, the sticker shock of three high-quality bathroom fans and a high-quality laundry room fan blurred my vision, so I purchased and installed cheap fans. The first time I turned any one of the fans on, I kicked myself. They all sounded like thrashing machines. Over the next few years, I replaced all three fans with the ones I should have bought in the first place. In each case, I had to tear out the bathroom ceilings and to replace the laundry room fan, I had to tear out part of a wall as well. Did I save any money overall? No.

Balancing function, aesthetics, and cost is difficult. First, forget the cost and look at what you're trying to achieve. Only after you define what you want, see if the project is within your budget. If not, then cuts will need to be made. Very important: look at the long-term cost. Do your best to "Crystal Ball" the future. If you do, you'll be happier with the results. Good luck and have fun.

Construction 101 -
Codes

Many of us bristle when it comes to government regulations. Some believe there are too many regulations, and I sometimes agree. But I sure wouldn't want to jump on an airplane if the Federal Aviation Administration (FAA) didn't regulate flights.

The same can be said for most building codes. Per Wikipedia, the purpose of building codes is to provide minimum standards for safety, health, and general welfare including structural integrity, mechanical integrity (including sanitation, water supply, light, and ventilation), means of egress, fire prevention and control, and energy conservation. These codes also set building standards that keep builders honest and help insurance companies know what they are insuring.

Most municipalities in the United States use the International Residential Code (IRC) for single or double-family occupied homes. However, other code standards might apply in your area. Check with the Building Department that has jurisdiction over your home before you build or remodel. A few calls to find out who is in charge of issuing permits and inspections could save you money and a few headaches. "An ounce of prevention in this case, is worth a pound of cure."

Depending on the type and scope of the handicap modifications you plan to make, you may or may not require a permit. And you may or may not be required to hire an architect or have the project engineered. Call first to see what is required.

As a retired building contractor, I recommend you follow the IRC, even if a permit is not required for your project and/or your municipality doesn't enforce codes. By following codes, you know that the project will be done correctly. It will be safe and can be insured. You also can also be more confident that you're not going to face unexpected obstacles when you or your loved one sells your home. I was often called to fix code violations found by a home inspector before a lender would finance the home's purchase.

So, as a consumer, how do you know if your contractor is following code? If the project is going to be inspected, you can reasonably think local codes are being followed. If your project doesn't require inspection, do a little homework. Many libraries and building departments have codebooks that you can borrow. Codebooks can be darned hard, even for the experts to interpret, but simple things you're likely to be concerned with can easily be found. Things like, how many outlets can be on a 20 amp circuit [10]? Or what is the maximum height of a stair [9.5"]? Or what is the maximum distance between balusters on a deck [4"]?

Now let's talk a little bit about the Americans with Disabilities Act (ADA). The ADA doesn't apply to single or even multiple family homes unless Federal money was used to construct the dwelling. For instance, the ADA might apply if Federal money was used to build a low-income apartment building. It doesn't apply to the remodel you're doing on your home. However, the ADA

Guidelines are an excellent place to start for ramps [no steeper than 12:1], or the height of a sink [34"] and mirror [top edge 74" from floor], or the width of a door [32"]. You won't go wrong if you do follow ADA Guidelines and, good news; you can Google almost any question you might have regarding the ADA.

Not convinced you should follow the code? A few years ago, I was waiting for the Building Inspector to inspect a project my company was working on. When he showed up a half-hour late, he apologized, saying he'd been in court most of the day. He'd been subpoenaed to testify for a plaintiff in a civil case. The plaintiff was hurt on a set of interior stairs that hadn't been built to code. Since the home was relatively new, the plaintiff won, and the homeowner's insurance company had to pay damages and legal fees.

The moral of the story; follow all applicable codes.

Construction 101 -
Outlets

Though this section is primarily theory, I'm including the overall discussion of outlets here.

Technically "outlets" are electrical receptacles, but most of us call them outlets.

To meet code in most of the US, an outlet is required every 12 feet in new residential construction. That means if you measure between outlets, that measurement must be under 12 feet. Knowing the code, and that there never seems to be an outlet where you want it, when my wife and I built our house, I installed an outlet every six feet; double the number required by code. Now I wish I had wired in a few more.

Unless you genuinely know what you're doing when it comes to electrical wiring, hire a licensed professional electrician. And be sure to tell that electrician to install lots and lots of outlets.

In the introduction to this section, I talked about the power and specialized outlets needed just at my desk. Think about your specific equipment and its needs when planning outlets.

Ramps

Perhaps the first modification to one's home to make life easier and safer for a pALS is the addition of a ramp or ramps. The desired angle of the ramp is 4 ¾ degrees or a 1 to 12 ratio; for every inch of rise, or fall, the run will 12 inches or one foot. So, if your porch is 2 feet higher than the sidewalk that leads to your home, a 24-foot-long ramp will be required for the ideal and safest angle of a 1:12 pitch.

Many homes will not have enough room for a 24-foot-long ramp. If this is your situation, you must double back, with landings between direction changes or increase the angle of your ramp. Ideally, you need 4-feet for the landing, so, the total length of your ramp including the landing, needs to be 28-feet long. While not ideal, even a slight increase in the ramp's angle will make a big difference. If you increase the pitch to a 1 ¼ to 12 ratio, you will shorten the ramp by almost five feet, which could make all the difference in fitting your ramp into the confines of your yard.

Here is a real-life example of a ramp build gone wrong. Gary, one of the guys in our ALS Men's group, hired a contractor to build a ramp from his front door to his driveway. The contractor was to build the ramp while Gary and his wife were away. Upon return, they found a well-constructed and nice-looking ramp, the bottom of which extended a couple of feet into their skinny driveway. They could barely fit their car past the ramp, and backing the car out of the driveway without hitting it was more of a challenge than his wife wanted to deal with. Worse, if the vehicle was parked in the driveway, it blocked the bottom of the ramp. The ramp had to be rebuilt with a slightly steeper pitch.

To avoid problems like Gary had, carefully layout the ramp to full scale in its precise location. Take a carpenter's stringline and stretch it from the top of the proposed ramp to the bottom. You can then visualize where the ramp will be, see if it will fit, and if you must alter the design. It is a lot easier to make changes before the ramp is built than after.

Also, before you start building the ramp, check all applicable building codes in your area [see Codes above]. And, just as important, know where all underground utilities are located. In the USA, call 811 to contact the underground utility locator in your area. "Better safe than sorry." That applies to utilities, codes, and making sure your ramp fits where you want it.

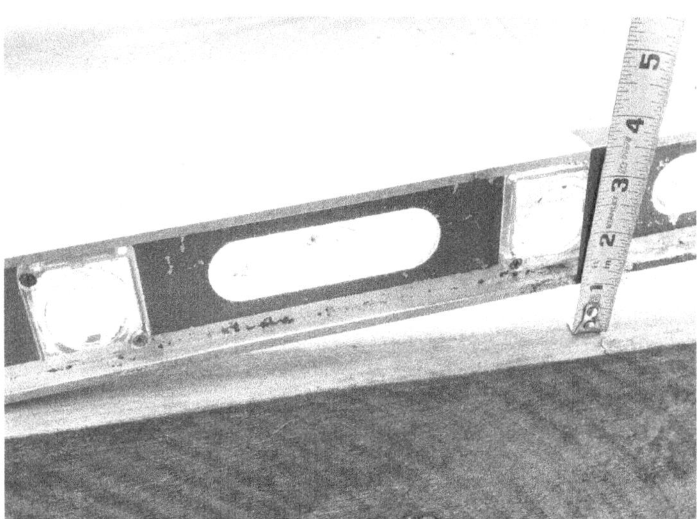

Checking for a 1" rise in 12" a 1:12 ratio.

Marcel heading up the ramp.

Bathroom Modifications

Right after ramps are are accommodations to the bathroom. A toilet might need to be raised, a shower significantly modified, a sink might need to be changed to be accessed from a wheelchair, and no doubt, grab bars will be required. Since everyone's disability is different and people vary in size, it is hard to generalize what modifications will be needed. One of my friends was diagnosed over five years ago with limb onset ALS. So far, his ALS only affects his shoulders and arms, so the only modification he has needed is to add a bidet seat to his toilet. A different friend diagnosed with limb onset ALS less than three years ago had to have a whole new bedroom and bathroom built. During the rebuild, he had a track mounted ceiling hoist installed that lifts him from his bed and transports him to the toilet or into the shower.

Bathrooms, too, need many outlets and these outlets should be separate from the bedroom outlet circuits. All bedrooms now require an Arc Fault Interrupt Breaker (AFCI), and bathrooms require a Ground Fault Circuit Interrupt (GFCI) circuit. Experts say AFCI breakers are not always compatible with GFCI outlets, so it's best to have them on different circuits.

Do your best to predict what will be required down the road when modifying your bathroom. Even as a contractor, I did a poor job predicting how my ALS would progress and what I'd need in my bathroom. So, I've had to make several modifications as time passed.

When it came to building and then redoing my bathroom, I did one thing wrong and one thing right. First, the wrong. I mounted the soap niche way too high for a person sitting on a shower chair. I was still able to stand when I mounted it, and never thought I'd have to sit to shower. The thing I did right was to nail ½ inch CDX plywood on the wall studs before I added any wall coverings like sheetrock or the acrylic shower surround. That plywood has allowed me to place grab bars anywhere I needed them as my ALS progressed. And I have a ton of grab bars in my bathroom; a dozen total, with seven of those dozen in the shower. We added most of the grab bars as my physical abilities declined, and may need to add at least one more.

More about plywood under the wall coverings. If you live in an area prone to tornados or earthquakes, you might want to make your bathroom into a Safe Room. If you are a wheelchair user, when your tornado siren goes off, it would be hard to access an underground shelter. Why not make your bathroom a place you can seek shelter during a natural disaster? You will already have easy and fast access to that room, and the small investment in plywood to cover the walls and ceiling could save your life.

Bathroom cabinet modification

Before modifications.

After modifications.

Bidets

Though I'm learning, I've made more than one mistake along the way. That's okay. I'd like others to learn from my mistakes.

1. If you are about to remodel your bathroom, be sure to have your electrician add an outlet behind the toilet.

2. If you're building a new house, again, have an outlet wired in behind your toilet. When I built our house in 2007, I did all the wiring and plumbing. Though I put a lot of thought into the placement of outlets, putting one behind a toilet never crossed my mind. And, worse, when I made it handicap accessible, again, I never thought about an outlet behind the toilet.

A few things I've learned from others about bidets.

1. Don't buy a cheap one, because it won't last.

2. If you don't want to freeze your tush off, you will want electric power to heat the water, and that the outlet needs to be protected by a GFCI outlet or breaker.

3. A heated seat is very nice, too. We pALS have a hard enough time staying warm without sitting on a cold toilet seat with our pants down.

4. One thing that came up at our local chapter of the ALSA Men's only meeting: consider getting a remote control for the bidet. That way, the caregiver doesn't have to help with the bidet controls. Plus, I find the remote control easier to reach than the side controls; I have both on my toilet seat bidet, and I never use the side controls.

They say a photo is worth a thousand words, so now to the pictures. We have two bathrooms on our main floor; a half-bath that my wife, Connie, uses and the ensuite bath off the main floor bedroom that I use. The two toilets are separated by a plumbing wall and are back-to-back. Connie wanted a bidet in her toilet, and since the bidet's instructions clearly say, "Don't use an extension cord," we had to run power to behind her toilet. We used surface-mount

Marcel LaPerriere

Wiremold and accessed power from my bathroom, as well as adding an outlet behind my toilet to power its bidet seat.

Since I'm confined to a wheelchair, and since my hands don't work all that well, Connie, under my direction, did all the work. And since I can't talk, I had to type instructions for her into my phone. Even though she has never done anything like this, she did a great job. I tell you; my wife is an amazing lady!

Connie getting ready to install a retro junction box for the wiring. That box will be for the outlet for her toilet in the ½ bath.

Wiring in the outlet that will feed power to both the ½ bath bidet and the bidet on my toilet. Note: The combined power draw of both bidets is under 15-amps, and the circuit is protected by a 20-amp breaker and a GFCI outlet located in my bathroom.

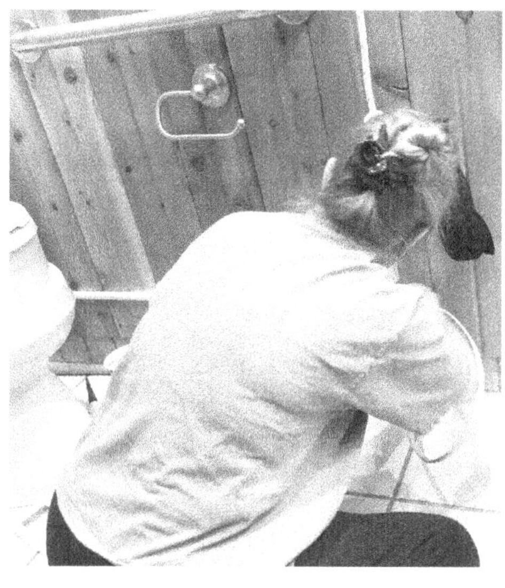

Feeding wire down the wire molding.

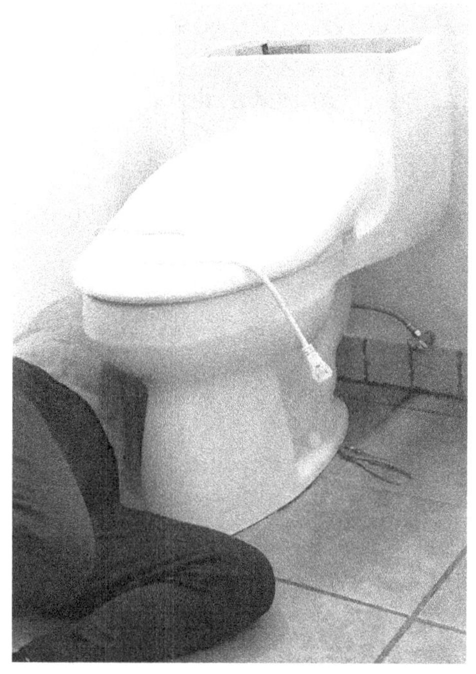

Installing the plumbing for the bidet in Con-nie's 1/2 bath.

The finished bidet toilet seat in the ½ bath.

An under-the-toilet riser and a bidet in-stalled on my toilet.

Bathroom Exhaust Fans

When the carpenter does the framing for a bathroom exhaust fan or the plumber hooks up the ducting, or even when the electrician hooks up the wiring, they often call the bathroom exhaust fan a fart fan. One of the fan's objectives is to get rid of the less than desirable odor but, unless you live in an extremely low humidity area, the fan's more critical function is to exhaust excess moisture.

Since ALS compromises the ability to breathe, we need to do all we can to improve air quality. Excess humidity is a breeding ground for molds and mildews, so we strive to replace moist air with ambient-humid air. Hence, the bathroom exhaust fan.

Choose a fan that can totally replace the bathroom air eight times in one hour when the bathroom is occupied or when humidity needs to be lowered. By computing the bathroom's square footage and looking at the cubic feet per minute (CFM) rating on the fan, we can select the proper fan. Ducting length and any ducting elbows will reduce the CFM's.

No one wants to hear a thrashing machine when the fan is turned on, so chose a quiet one. The Sone Rating rates noise output; the lower the Sones, the more silent the fan. A quiet, high-quality fan costs more, but it is money well spent.

I like Panasonic fans. Of their dozens of styles, surely one will meet your needs. I also like to control the fan with a Leviton humidity sensing switch with a built-in timer. Besides being able to turn the fan on or off manually, the Leviton switch will turn the fan on and off pending the humidity level. This kind of control costs more than a simple on/off switch, or timer, but, it's worth the extra money to ensure the fan runs when it needs to run.

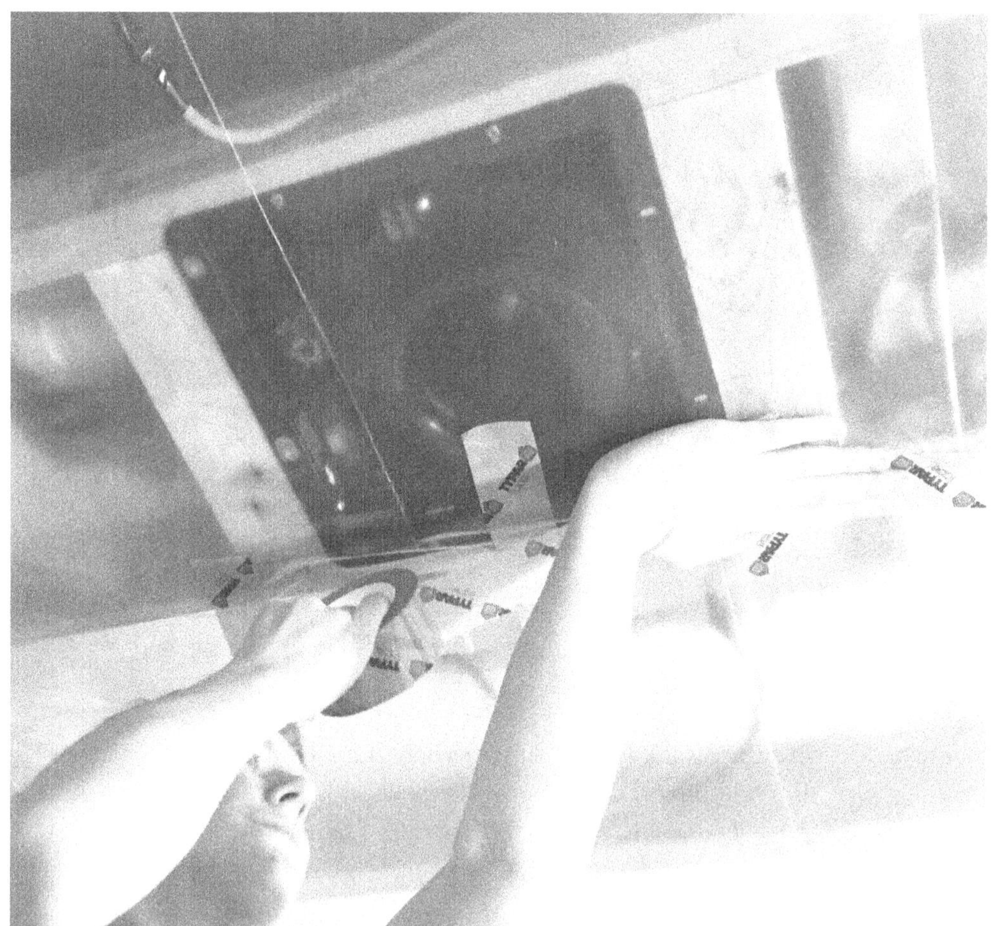

Under my directions, my 17-year-old grandson, Blake installs a new bathroom fan and the plastic vapor barrier in my handicap-accessible bathroom. The round wires are for low voltage LED lights.

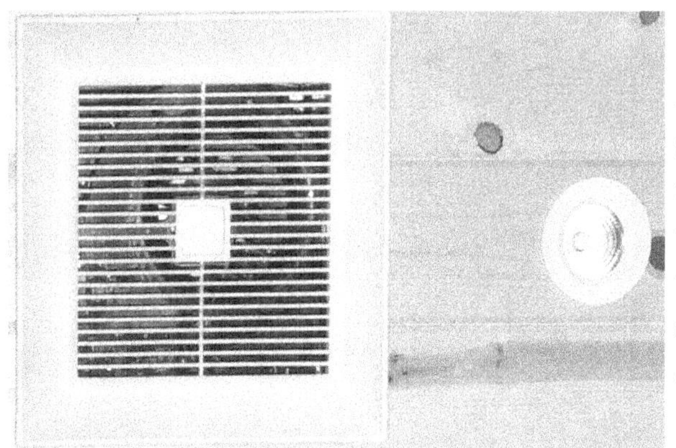

Since we had a 9-foot ceiling in my bathroom, when we did modifications for my disability, we lowered the ceiling to 8' 6" which made it easy to install a quiet fan and low voltage LED lighting.

Next to the light switch is a humidity sensor switch. If the humidity gets too high, the fan will turn on for 30-minutes. The fan switch can also be manually controlled, and once turned on, it will automatically shut off after 30-minutes.

Bedroom Modifications

When it comes to modifying a bedroom for someone with ALS, the question most commonly asked on Facebook support sites is what type of flooring to use. People respond recommending everything from hardwood to ceramic tile, and some even say carpet. I'm biased against carpet; I hate it. As to "What type of flooring works best?" "It depends on several factors."

We have to go back to budget, function, and aesthetics. Let's take those one at a time.

Budget. Flooring, like all modifications, is expensive. That's why some folks like carpet. Generally speaking, carpet is the least expensive flooring option. But when we factor in function; carpet fails miserably. The house my wife, son, and I built has in-floor radiant heat. The last thing we'd want for efficient heat transfer is carpet. And carpet sucks when it comes to rolling a manual wheelchair or anything manually pushed on wheels. When I was first losing my ability to walk and climb stairs, I could still use a non-motorized wheelchair. We took a close to three-month road trip, staying in a different hotel most nights. With one exception, every night, we stayed in handicap-accessible rooms. That handicap-room was on the 2nd floor in a hotel with no elevator. But I digress.

During that trip, I rolled my wheelchair on different carpets almost every night. Some carpets were okay, okay with a thumbs down, and some were impossible, which required being pushed by Connie. Each night I'd enter the hotel room in my 405 pound, Permobil F3, knowing I'd have to transfer to my manual wheelchair because of the confined space. The first thing I'd look at was the flooring, and if I saw plush carpet, I'd utter several cuss words to myself. Some of those carpets were aesthetically pleasing, but they rate low functionally. Ironically, the one-room big enough for me to stay in my F3 had an aesthetically pleasing and fine functioning ceramic tile floor. That hotel was located just a few feet from a sandy beach, and I'm sure it helped save on the hotel's cleaning budget.

So, what flooring is best? There are too many factors to make a generalized statement. I rate ceramic tile highest in most cases. Had I known seven short years after we built our house in 2007 I'd start the ALS downward spiral, I would have used ceramic tile with a thin grout line. I would have installed a simulated wood pattern of 8-inch by 48-inch tiles on all the floors in the main living area. It would have been more durable and easier to keep clean than the wood flooring we chose.

One step down from ceramic tile would be pre-finished solid hardwood flooring. Like ceramic tile, hardwood flooring is expensive, so, if you have a tight budget, consider engineered wood floors. Engineered wood floors are not as durable as solid wooden floors. Another durable floor that may be less expensive than those I've mentioned, is vinyl click-lock flooring. And if your bedroom happens to be built on a concrete slab, you could leave the floor unfinished. That might not aesthetically pleasing, but its durable and easy on the pocketbook.

I also like vinyl tile. It has the industrial look of a school or hospital floor, but it's used in large high-traffic buildings because it's inexpensive, very durable, and easy to clean. And, other than bare concrete, it's the easiest to install of all flooring options.

Now that I have ALS, outlets in the bedroom are even more important than they were before. Since I must have my head elevated to breathe, I need a hospital bed. And speaking of breathing, I depend on my Trilogy Ventilator, which uses two outlets. Then, there is a light on my nightstand and a very dim night-light plugged into the wall. Plus, two clocks, sometimes a wheelchair charger and a cough-assist machine. Also, an electric blanket. I have a lot of trouble rolling over, so heavy blankets aren't an option. The electric blanket keeps me warm. That's nine outlets if the hospital bed is not electric.

Necessary modern medical equipment requires many many outlets. Over a dozen years ago when designing the electrical system for our house and pulling the wires, I never imagined I'd need the number of outlets for all the medical gadgets that keep me alive.

So, if you are starting, working on, or will soon work on making your house to make it more accessible for a handicapped person, please don't overlook the necessity of lots of outlets. One 20-amp circuit should cover a bedroom's needs but two would be better.

When modifying a bedroom, there are many other considerations. One often-overlooked thing is soundproofing. As poorly as I sleep nowadays, I wish my bedroom had a better barrier to outside noises. We recently had the glass changed from double-pane to triple-pane glass in my bedroom windows. It's incredible what one more thin piece of glass can make in mitigating outside noise. Again, had I been able to see the future, I would have added at least an inch of foam insulation board under the sheetrock in addition to the fiberglass insulation packed between the studs. With foam insulation and three panes of glass, the room wouldn't let in many outside sounds and I would sleep better.

One thing I like about my small bedroom is the closets. One, about eight-foot-wide with bi-fold doors, is where we store the Hoyer Lift and my limited hanging wardrobe. Across the room next to the bathroom door is a two-foot-wide closet with a bi-fold door and shelves. I can easily reach my clothing we store there from my wheelchair. One shelf is dedicated to underwear and socks, one to pants, and one to T-shirts, and there is still plenty of room for other daily necessities. The shelves that are too high for me to reach are the home for spare bedding.

We built this bathroom attached to the bedroom; called ensuite in most Western counties outside of the US. The bathroom is such an essential part of my care; I have no idea how other pALS do without an ensuite bathroom. Transferring me from the toilet to the bed and back would be very very difficult if they weren't as close together as they are.

I'm also delighted that during our house design, I was adamant that all exterior and interior doors had to 36-inches wide. My wheelchair wouldn't fit through narrower doors. My bathroom door opened just a bit past 90 degrees, which made navigating my chair or the standing lift from the bedroom into the bathroom difficult. One of my grandsons removed the door solving that problem. Since my wife is my caretaker, privacy wasn't a concern when we removed the door. If privacy is an issue, consider a pocket or sliding barn door. No door is easy to open or close when sitting in a wheelchair, so though they are not cheap, an automatic sliding or opening door is an option.

Other things that make life easier are voice-activated light switches and other types of smart controls in your bedroom. We don't have those convinces in my room, but we do have a three-way switch by the bed to control three wall-sconce lights. Thus, those three lights can be turned on when entering the bedroom and off from the bed, or vice versa. And since those lights are wall-mounted, they don shine in one's eyes when lying in bed. There are also two overhead and much brighter lights that can be turned on for cleaning or whenever more lighting is desired.

I've written over 1400-words, and I still haven't told you about my bed, the whole reason for a bedroom. Because Medicare has a limit on what bed they will pay for, I have an Invacare, hospital-type bed. Just because it is inexpensive doesn't mean it isn't functional and comfortable. After we added a convoluted foam mattress topper, it may be the most comfortable hospital bed

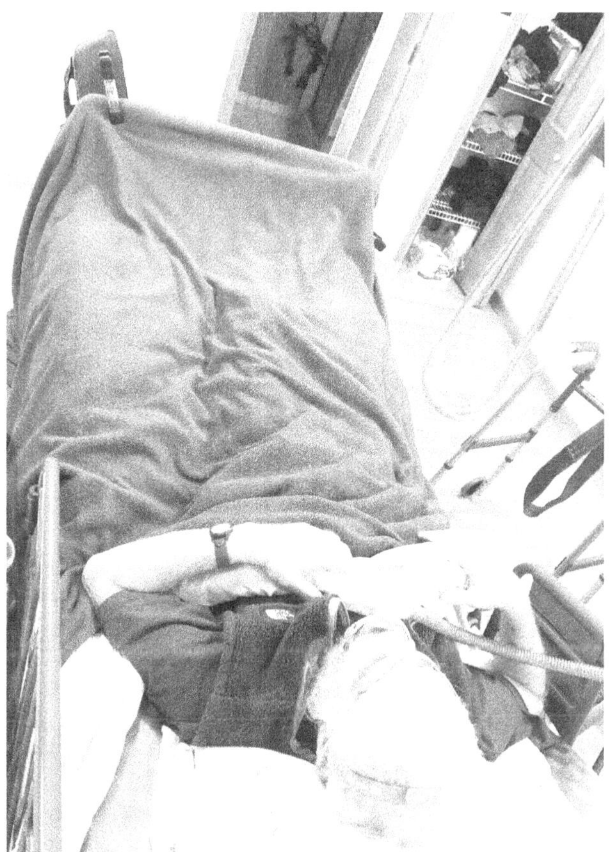

An electric blanket keeps me warm and toasty.

I've ever slept in. But the squeaks from the frame and springs drove my poor wife crazy, to the point she moved her bed into the living room. You get what you pay for. Since Medicare and our insurance paid for it, we couldn't expect it to be a nice as a $5,000.00 bed that you'd typically see in an American hospital.

True to our pattern, we modified it to better fit my needs. First, Connie made satin lower sheets, which help her pivot my legs when she lifts them into bed. Plus, the soft satin helps reduce the chance of abrasion pressure sores. Next, to stay warm without piling on a ton of blankets, we added an electric blanket. After two different electric blankets failed in a short amount of time, we bought a Serta brand electric blanket, which is still working after two years. The Serta blanket has ten different heat settings and a built-in timer to shut it off. If I'm just slightly chilled, I might set it at the lowest heat with the

A plywood board at the foot of the bed keeps the weight of the blankets off my feet, helping reduce the chances of pressure sores.

timer set for 30 minutes. But if I'm shiveringly cold, I can set it on high for a couple of hours. To minimize downward pressure on my feet, we extended the footboard up with a piece of plywood. By draping the blankets over the footboard extension, my feet are more or less under a blanket tent, which also helps with pressure sores.

As of this writing, in June of 2021, I can still sometimes transfer from my bed into my wheelchair and back. A couple of things make that possible. There are two trapeze poles attached to the headboard that extends over my head. From those hang webbing straps that enable me to pull myself partially up, which assists enough to allow my legs to pivot off the bed. Once I'm sitting on the side of the bed, there is a floor-to-ceiling pole which allows me to stand and rotate 90 degrees into my chair. Unfortunately more and more, I depend on Connie to lift me in and out of bed with our Invacare standing electric lift. That takes me back full circle to floor coverings. Since my petit wife weighs between sixty or seventy pounds less than I do, a hard surface floor is imperative when it comes to her pushing the lift. Without wood on the bedroom floor and ceramic tile on the bathroom floor, it would be impossible for her to push the lift with me in it. That's why I'm not fond of even the lowest nap carpet.

Webbing hangs for the trapeze poles. I like to hang the hose from my Trilogy noninvasive ventilator from a carabiner hanging from webbing. From that same carabiner are the controls for the electric blanket. The cloth hanging over the Trilogy screen keeps the light from the screen from lighting up my bedroom at night. The screen auto-darkens after three minutes, but it never completely darkens until it is reset, and if I sneeze, that sneeze causes a momentary alarm. At the lower right is one of two spring clamps that hold the blankets off my feet and the vertical wood handrail.

Another modification we made to the bed shortly after we got it was to add a vertical five-foot-long piece of handrail to the footboard. That vertical pole made it possible for me to stand, which enabled Connie to pull my pants up when she dresses me. Now that we have the floor-to-ceiling steel pole, we use the wooden pole only if a silly little dog decides to lie down in front of the metal pole while I'm being dressed. It's handy to have another pole I can fall back on. (*BTW: Silly dogs or cats are also good additions when making modifications to your home. They help tamp down the frustration of having to rely on something you didn't have to in the past.*)

We recently added two cordless doorbell buttons so I can summon Connie's help. One is on to the bed railing and the other I can reach from the toilet.

Life will be easier if you make proper modifications. Do your best to figure out what you need now and what you're going to need in the future. My short list: a hard surface floor, 36-inch-wide doors, closets where you can reach things when sitting in a wheelchair, and, if you are a light sleeper, soundproofing. Good luck and have some fun during the modification process.

Bird Drawings of Connie LaPerriere

Introduction

Over the years Connie has made hundreds of drawings, but I especially love her bird drawings. Although these drawings have no intrinsic connection to the collection of my essays cataloguing my ALS adventures, I want to include them here reaffirming her art and the enduring joy art gives us throughout our lives. May you enjoy them as I do.

2021. The wall in the LaPerriere home displaying Connie's drawings.

White Breasted Nuthatch

Bald Eagle.

Blue Heron.

Puffin.

Cormorant dries its wings.

Parker the raven.

Peregrine Falcon.

Red Breasted Sapsucker.

Two puffins knock heads.

Anna's hummingbird.

Black Capped Chickadee.

Marcel LaPerriere

Blue Heron.

Chickadee.

Downey Woodpecker.

Junco.

King Fisher.

Loon.

Northern Cardinal.

Pine Grosbeak.

Robin.

Sandpiper.

Marcel LaPerriere

Saw-whet Owl.

Seagull.

Two Bald Eagles.

Acknowledgements

Once again I owe Dana Anderson a big thank you for her professional work compiling my essays and putting them into this book. Dana did such a great job with my other books, *Just Another Adventure: Living with Amyotrophic Lateral Sclerosis (ALS)*, *The Adventure Continues: Living with Amyotrophic Lateral Sclerosis (ALS)*, and *The Road to Adventure,* that I was thrilled when she said she'd do this book, too.

Thanks, also, to Max and Bonnie Cottrell for proofreading many of these essays and Margot Demarais for the read-through and corrections.

The biggest thank you needs to go to my wife, Connie, who is always the first to read my writing and is always the first to make suggestions and correct my endless mistakes.

Thank you all; I couldn't have done it without your help.

About the Author

Like many Alaskans, Marcel worked in a magnitude of jobs. Those jobs included machinist, powerhouse mechanic, climbing and fitness gym owner, and owner of a web hosting service and online retail store that sold Alaska-made arts and crafts, logger and sawmill operator, carpenter, and director maintenance at a small liberal arts college, and a building contractor. He even did a year-long stint as a recruiter, traveling the state of Alaska looking for candidates for placement in a maritime academy. Not one to shy away from a challenge, Marcel thrived on hard work and hard play. He was an active scuba diver, logging over a thousand dives, a climber, a caver; with his wife, Connie, helped discover, explore, and map many caves in Southeast Alaska.

As ALS started to creep into Marcel's life, he elected to look at the disease as just another adventure, one that had been forced on him. He and Connie decided early on to do all they could to fight ALS, but accepted that an ALS diagnosis, at this time, is always a death sentence. They decided to make the most of each day and live life happy to accept the horrific disease that ALS is. As Marcel lost his ability to speak, he started writing. His books include *Just Another Adventure: Living with Amyotrophic Lateral Sclerosis (ALS)*, *The Adventure Continues: Living with Amyotrophic Lateral Sclerosis (ALS)*, and his book of true-life short stories, *The Road to Adventure*. He is currently working on a book about sailing and the twenty-five years he and Connie lived on sailboats.

Today he, Connie, and their beagle, Bella, live in a house that Connie, their son Zach, and he built in Sitka, Alaska.